"*Blessed as We Were* showcases poems rooted in place that barrel forward, leaving the reader gasping to take a breath by the end of each one. . . . [Gerald] Stern's selected poems showcase how language can create movement. They drive fast and hard and catalogue everything they can along the way."
— Elizabeth Deanna Morris Lakes, *Jewish Book Council*

"One of our most influential and beloved poets, fifty years after the publication of his first book, Gerald Stern is still in love, still angry, still outraged, and still funny. For Stern, every grief is personal and even a worm's death is worthy of justice. He is the lover of poets, friends, the homeless, animals, art, birds, flowers, grasses, trees, a witness of the holy sparks buried in the physical world, and a hater of lechers, liars, and hypocrites. His poetry is a devotion that rides the pure music of the heart. *Blessed as We Were* is the expression of a full life of loving, a crowning achievement, the luminous offering of an American original."
— Toi Derricotte

PRAISE FOR GERALD STERN

"The gratitude we feel toward Gerald Stern's work doesn't just have to do with his originality. . . . Perhaps it's listening in amazement as he resurrects our histories for us to sing; perhaps it's how he finds the joy in our grief, the unexpected ecstasies inhabiting the mundane. . . . Stern is one of those rare poetic souls who makes it almost impossible to remember what our world was like before his poetry came to exalt it."
— C. K. Williams

"[Stern's is] a mind that dances, prances, leaps and falls, and leaps again, through all of Western culture and history, all of its cities, many of its composers and violinists, all of its thinkers, and all of its prophets—of whom he is one."
— Alicia Ostriker

"There has never been a poet like Gerald Stern, who likes to shake things and empty them out, and then share what's found with the entire congregation. Sorrow and exultation get their equal turn, but it's the human imagination and all its jubilant fecundity that's paid special attention."
— Philip Schultz

"In every overcaffeinated and rumbustious line, Gerald Stern has been telling us that the best way to live is not so much for poetry but through poetry."
—David Kirby, *New York Times Book Review*

"[Stern] relished the particularities of reality and reverie alike, revelling in the mundane as well as the surreal. Over the decades, his work's idiosyncratic music heightened, celebrating the ever more marvellous accumulation of experience."
—Hannah Aizenman, *The New Yorker*

Blessed
as We
Were

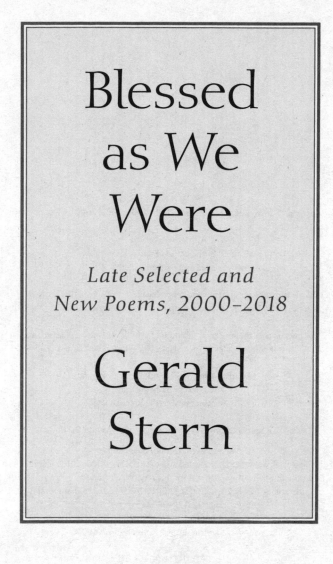

Blessed as We Were

Late Selected and New Poems, 2000–2018

Gerald Stern

W. W. NORTON & COMPANY
Celebrating a Century of Independent Publishing

For information about permission to reproduce selections from this book, write to
Permissions, W. W. Norton & Company, Inc., 500 Fifth Avenue, New York, NY 10110

For information about special discounts for bulk purchases, please contact
W. W. Norton Special Sales at specialsales@wwnorton.com or 800-233-4830

Manufacturing by Lakeside Book Company
Book design by JAM Design
Production manager: Lauren Abbate

Library of Congress Cataloging-in-Publication Data

Names: Stern, Gerald, date– author.
Title: Blessed as we were : late selected and new poems, 2000–2018 / Gerald Stern.
Description: First edition. | New York, NY : W. W. Norton & Company, [2020]
Identifiers: LCCN 2019036827 | ISBN 9781324002338 (hardcover) |
ISBN 9781324002345 (epub)
Classification: LCC PS3569.T3888 A6 2020 | DDC 811/.54—dc23
LC record available at https://lccn.loc.gov/2019036827

ISBN 978-1-324-06451-0 pbk.

W. W. Norton & Company, Inc., 500 Fifth Avenue, New York, N.Y. 10110
www.wwnorton.com

W. W. Norton & Company Ltd., 15 Carlisle Street, London W1D 3BS

1 2 3 4 5 6 7 8 9 0

For Anne Marie, whether in snow or sun. Always.

Contents

from In Beauty Bright (2012)

from Divine Nothingness (2015)

from Galaxy Love (2017)

from
Last Blue

One of the Smallest

Made of the first gray light
that came into my room,
made of the hole itself
in the cracked window blind,
thus made of sunshine, thus made of
gas and water, one of the
smallest, smallest, made of
that which seizes the eye,
that which an eagle needs
and even a mole, a mole, a
rabbit, a quail, a lilac,
it was uncreated. I
fought for it, I tore down
walls, I cut my trees,
I lay on my back, I had a
rock to support my head, I
swam in two directions,
I lay down smiling, the sun
made my eyes water, what
the wind and the dirt took away
and what was abraded and what was
exhausted, exhausted, was only
a just reflection. The sun
slowly died and I much
quicker, much quicker, I raced
until I was wrinkled but I was
lost as the star was and I
was losing light, I was dying
before I was born, thus I was
blue at the start, though I was
red much later, much later,
for I was a copy, but I was
something exploding and I was

born for just that but fought
against it, against it. The light
of morning was gray with a green
and that of evening was almost a
rose in one sky though it was
white in another—at least
in one place the light comes back—
and I disappeared like a fragment
of gas you'd call it, or fire,
fragment by fragment I think,
cooled down and changed into metal,
captured and packaged as it will be
in one or two more centuries
and turned then into a bell—
not a bridge, not a hammer—
really the tongue of a bell,
if bells will still be in use then,
and I will sing as a bell does,
you'd call it tolling—such
was my burst of light seen from
a certain viewpoint though seen from
another, another, no sudden
flash but a long slow burning
as in the olive tree burning,
as in the carob, as slow as the
olive, still giving up chocolate
after two thousand years, that's
what we lacked, our light
was like the comet's, like a
flash of fosfur, a burst
from a Spanish matchbox, the wood
broken in two, the flame
lasting six seconds—I counted—
that is, when the fosfur worked,
two or three lives lived out
in a metal ashtray, one of them

nothing but carbon, one of them
wood partway, poor thing that
died betimes, one snuffed out
just at the neck where the pinkish
head was twisted the wrong way
and one of them curling up
even after burning, thus the
light I loved stacked in a box
depending on two rough sides
and on the wind and on the
gentleness of my hand,
the index finger pressed
against the wood, the flash
of fire always a shock,
always new and enlightening,
the same explosion forever—
I call it forever—forever—
sitting with my mouth open
in some unbearable blue,
bridal wreath in my right hand,
since this is the season, my left hand
scratching and scratching, the sun
in front now. How did dogwood
get into this yard? How did
the iris manage to get here?
And grow that way? I live
without a beard, I'm streaked
with a kind of purple, my hands
are folded and overlapping, I
love the rain, I am
a type of Persian, where I am
and in this season I blossom
for fifteen hours a day, I
walk through streams of some sort—
I like that thinking—corpuscles
bombard my eyes—I call it

light—it was what gave me
life in the first place—no no
shame in wandering, no shame
in adoring—what it what it
was was so primitive
we had to disturb it—call it
disturbing, call it interfering—
at five in the morning in front of
the dumpster, at six looking down
on the river, a little tired from
the two hundred steps, my iris
in bloom down there, my maples
blowing a little, I was
a mole and a rabbit, I was
a stone at first, I turned
garish for a while and burned.

Pluma

Once, when there were no riches, somewhere in southern
Mexico I lost my only pen in the
middle of one of my dark and flashy moments
and euchred the desk clerk of my small hotel
out of his only piece of bright equipment
in an extravagance of double-dealing,
nor can I explain the joy in that and how I
wrote for my life, though unacknowledged, and clearly
it was unimportant and I had the money and
all I had to do was look up the Spanish and
I was not for a second constrained and there was
no glory, not for a second, it had nothing to
do with the price of the room, for example, it only
made writing what it should be and the life we
led more rare than what we thought and tested
the art of giving back, and someplace near me,
as if there had to be a celebration
to balance out the act of chicanery,
a dog had started to bark and lights were burning.

Against the Crusades

Don't think that being a left-handed nightingale was all legerdemain
or that I am that small angry bastard who hates whores,
only I disguised it by laughing; or that it's
easy leaving a restaurant by yourself and holding
your other hand against the bricks to keep from falling;
or anybody can play the harp, or anybody knows the words
to "Blue Sunday" and "After the Ball Was Just Over You Dropped Dead."

If you can stand Strauss then so can I,
oh filthy Danube, oh filthy Delaware, oh filthy Allegheny.

And anyone who never opened a Murphy bed
night after night for seven years without ripping
the sheet and had neither desk nor dresser can't walk
in my shoes or wear my crocodile T-shirt.
And anyone thinking that a Jew being a Jew
is something you should apologize for as if Richard
Wagner just stepped into the room wearing a bronze
headpiece with a pink feather sticking out of it
is nothing less than a fool himself who buys into
dead stoves and dead feelings and doesn't know the
sweetness of his own lips and the tenderness of his fingers.

God bless the Jewish comedians who never denigrated Blacks,
and God bless the good gentiles and God bless Mayor Scully
and Councilman Wolk and Rosey Rowswell and Eleanor Roosevelt;
and the chorus of Blue Saints behind Bishop Elder Beck
and the old theater on Wylie Avenue I visited every Sunday night
to hear them sing and pray and hear him preach.

God bless the Lucca Cafe. God bless the green benches
in Father Demo Square and the dear Italian lady
carrying a huge bouquet of red and white roses
in front of her like a candelabra and the tiny white
baby's breath that filled the empty spaces with clapping and singing.

Someone to Watch Over Me

It is not knowing what a mulberry sidewalk looks like
in the first place that will start you up sliding, then dancing,
though if it weren't for my bird-like interior and how I shake
one foot then the other I would have not seen the encroachment
myself; and if it weren't for the squirrel who lives in pure greed
and balances whatever he touches with one hand then another
I would have picked the berries up one berry at a time
and laid them out to dry beside my crinkled lily and my pink daisy.
In this decade I am taking care of the things I love. I'm
sorting everything out starting, if I have to, with the
smallest blossom, the smallest, say, salmon-colored petunia.
I'm eating slowly, dipping one crumb at a time in my beer,
and singing—as I never did before—one word at a time
in my true voice, which is after all a quiet second tenor
that came upon me after my first descent into manhood
and after a disgrace involving my seventh-grade music teacher
and a sudden growth of hair. If it weren't for my large lips
I could have played the French horn. If I didn't like mulberries—
one among a million, I know, and eat them—without sugar—
the way a grackle does his from the downtrodden branches
I wouldn't be standing on a broken chair, and I wouldn't be shaking;
and if I didn't slide from place to place and walk
with a toothbrush in my pocket and touch one bush
for belief and one for just beauty I wouldn't be singing.

Wailing

Walking from west to east past the living
dead man on the corner of Grove and Fourth
north side of the bank I closed my eyes
so I wouldn't have to see his stumps and the red
mouth without a tongue and make the water
rush through my ears so I wouldn't have to hear him.

And sitting on the bench across the street
I exchanged ideas with the woman next to me
on a question in ethics, Kant and Schlegel; I made
a reference to early Herodotus, she stuck by
Bentham, pleasure and pain, though she was loyal
also to Hobbes, he of the loathsome universe.

While the sun, though who would notice it, was covered
in what the older Plato would call slime
and the one tree that didn't have metal growing
through it shook with life—I'd say it was leaves
but birds rushed by and one was Bentham and one
was Hobbes himself, one of the true slime-chasers.

And sitting across from me although the lice
drove him crazy was the master of nuance
lifting a wing and eating, he of the blinking
eyes we waited for standing alone
and walking along the slats of his bench, the prince
of bleeding mouths, I'm sure, and duke of welts,

not to mention organs erupting and faces
some black and some red but all with huge creases and I,
with a scholar like that, I kept him in bread, I gave him
one Guggenheim after another, even I
gave him a Hobbes, a half a bagel, with seeds
from the opium tree and did my drumming, hands

11

on the cement armrests, now beginning to clap,
and a tongue of my own inside my mouth, still thinking,
still talking, I will learn to forgive, still lucky
to have a tongue and sit in New York and bleed
only a little, from one or two cuts, and lucky
to walk the way I do and have my own secret

and shoulder my bag as I get up and walk
to another part of the city, past, I'm sure,
shoes and wine and futons, thinking up
a plan for not eating, a place for my papers, a room
to read in, a chair to live in my next two years
and keep my tongue intact, poor suffering mouth

at the corner of Fourth and Grove, and lie down hard
when I have to and sit where I want and wait for my own
restaurant to open and drink my coffee at last
in a certain park, at another bench, this one
with curved iron sides in stamped black: fruit and flowers
and yellow lacquered slats, a bench for wailing,

with a name on it in English and even dates
for someone to study and only three short lines
to memorize, the plate attached with bolts
from front to back, the metal treated, a rat
for witness, a sparrow to eat the pizza, a *Times*
to sit on, a daughter for whistling, a mother for staring,

and someone to loosen the bolts and someone to stand
in front of me with a flute and throw his hat
on a little Turkish rug and someone to sit
beside me and wail, "coffee from 1940,"
"pie from 1936," the only
song I know, half Mississippi, half Poland.

His Cup

His song was only a dot—a flash—if anything,
somewhere above that haze which he remembered,
when he thought about it, as a world on fire
or a white mind watching. When he shook his cup
there was a tremor, something like a distant
coruscation, he knew this and his own mind
was always either on that or on the sky
north of his grandmother's house and the long building
they called the forge and the 1939 Chevy
with the gray metal visor and the sweet acorn
with the spiked helmet. He remembered a pig
burning in sand and how they hunted all day
for the two hot eyes, and he remembered floating
under the wire they stretched across the creek
and holding his breath. The violin star is closest,
the trombone star is farthest—or the drum star—
depending on what he sang. He worked this out,
some ratio or other, forty years ago
in order to learn how music worked. If there
was an analogue for what he did it was a
nova exploding in front of the Chemical Bank,
a state of mind of the millionth brightness, his cup
gone wild, the light spilling—nothing
could take that from him. He ate from a leather case
and slept where he worked; he put quarters in one pocket
and dimes in another. As far as a change of belief,
as far as the red and the blue, as far as abortion
and standing armies and cheaper health care, even as
far as the final outburst, he was silent—
dumb, you'd say—that was the evil of music
as well as the good; and twice he changed his corner,
and once he left his cup where it was and started
howling, what else could you call it? Moaning,

hissing even, such was the light there and such
was the uncreated light. He ended up
somewhere between a rubbing and scraping, maybe
a kind of sucking, but mostly he plucked, for plucking
was how he explained it, he was both singing and plucking
and dust and gases were collecting for he was
thinking of something else, oh, prairie schooners
fording the creek, the raging channel against
the farther side; and justice again, that which
confounded it from the beginning, and he was
dying to taste those pork chops and walk the fences
between the cows, and he was dying to feed them
and watch them eat; and in the second brain,
for it is always the second brain that makes
the lucid sounds, or so he reasoned, he watched
himself in a black suit seated at a score
on a polished stage with pipes behind him and baffles
to the left and right, his shoes polished, the light
shining on the wood, a rapt audience
of college students in rags and older professionals
and businesspeople ready to leap to their feet
and shout for him, but he just finished the piece
on a long slow note and waited for the last
invisible sound and then two seconds of silence
before he rose and entered that thunder, his mind
already on the next great piece, how this time
the strings would fly more and the lights would burst
without stopping, or put it this way, there would
be a desert and he would walk till the blood
was almost gone and he would be a thrasher
with only two sharp sounds, or he would play
the first instrument, something to do with slapping
and something with whistling. He was grateful to the woman
who kept applauding, he bowed to her, he did
that dumb kissing with his hand, only finding
a ratio between the two, the sound of kissing,

the sound of clapping—she would give him a dollar
if she were passing by his bank, the light
was on her and she *was* the light; like him
she made it appear and disappear, her clapping
in tune with his kissing, in an empty hall
of maybe three hundred seats—they were the last
and walked into the parking lot, a single
Plymouth was there, the moon was full, the frogs
were at it again, such melody, and such, such
gruesome rhythm—he loved all frogs—his head
was in her lap, the car was moving, the cup
was spilling again, this was his major explosion.

Greek Neighbor Home from the Hospital

Where he hung the bird feeder a month ago
a kind of film is covering the thin glass
and where he threw his wine glass down a bleeding heart
is starting to show under the motherly leaves.

He has walked to the wire fence three times
to study my tomatoes and he has smelled
my roses in a downward movement in which
his good leg was one anchor and his cane another.

I can tell by the clicks of triumph and the loud
rattle of his newspaper the Russians
have sold missiles to the Greek Cypriots
and Turkey is going to suffer. As I recall

he put the key to the padlock in the pot
of new lettuce and I can see his glasses
under his chair in case he panics. The wind
makes both of us smile a little and the swallows

for just a second seem to lounge, the sky
is so blue, they almost rest. He leaves his chair
by twirling; he hates their rectitude, and since
the dog is dead, and since his wife went to live

with her daughter again he closes the door by himself
and either sits in the kitchen and falls asleep
over his cane or climbs his eighteen stairs
before he turns the light on—I'll know which

by the count of thirty, either one of which,
to my way of thinking, is better than the brutal
battles they had, at least for my own sleep
over the honey locust, before his stroke

a month ago in front of the glass feeder
separating the different kinds of birdseed
into their small compartments without giving
too much away to the poisonous squirrels, poor Greek.

Pennsylvania Bio

I wore a black knit hat
so I could be undistinguished in the war
and carried a small bag
so I could be mistaken for a doctor;

and once in a whorehouse
while waiting for a friend of mine to finish
I examined the madam on the kitchen table;
and I spent Sunday at either the Serbian Club

or the postwar Literary Club on Atwood Street
above the prewar clothing store, and ate
hot sausage sandwiches and cold buttermilk
across the street from the first Carnegie Library

and made plans for the next seventy years. I drove
Andy Warhol to the East Liberty train station
in my father's 1949 Ford. Believe it or
not I bought a 1950 Buick

thirteen years later for fifteen dollars and drove it
into a junkyard five years after. My first
instrument was a kind of kazoo and that led
naturally to a golden trombone. I was

loyal to my own music for fifty years
though I detested snare drums and tap dancing,
just as I do those singers now who hold
their left fists in the air while holding the microphone

inside their mouths. And I hate short-sleeved shirts
when they wear them with dark neckties, skinny swine
knocking on closed doors; and I had a habit
of counting bricks, a nice obsession compared to

washing hands or touching car doors, it gave me
freedom with walls so I could handle bulging
and sagging when I had to; and one of the summers
I read Steinbeck and made love—in the bedroom—

to my aunt's cleaning woman in upstate Pennsylvania
and learned to adore the small town with its rows
of stores and trees on the sidewalk and only a short walk
into the country, in this case up a steep hill,

the dogs more sullen the farther up you went,
and Russian and Roman churches below, the sunlight
on the river, the bridge empty, the outer one
half-hidden, I was shocked by the sudden distance,

and I had a Brown's Beach jacket with a reddish
thorn in one of the pockets, which was my toothpick
for thirty-five years, and a vest to match, and a flattened
acorn I kept in the darkness; and I had a pencil

I used to keep my balance, the edges were eaten,
the lead was gray, the green eraser was worn
down to the metal, and I had a spiral notebook
I kept for emotions, and I folded my money.

Massachusetts Song

That is the education of a tree,
one stick by which morality, aesthetics,
music, and politics are taught,
whether a pecan or plum;

and that the wire,
although I hate to mention the wire,
and reddish apples and limbs so low
they drag on the ground;

and that the confluence where
five branches start, a university
hard by the lonely peach;
and that a nest for the bluebird,

a wooden box with a hole
too small for the sparrow;
and that is the loaded branch of the pitch pine where
I saw the perfect body and heard the song

in secret oh I swear you swallows I swear
you sunlight on the salt grass what the blue jay
called silence what the rose hip
and the dead raccoon called home you crows.

A Rose Between the Sheets

Taffeta for you and taffeta for me, a rose
between the sheets and one sitting on my finger
as if it were a ruben-stein; a dress
you held once in your arms against your face
and one I lifted over your waist and spread
like a noisy pillow; you in your silk and me
in my leather jacket, nothing else, raw silk
for you, cowhide for me, and velvet
on your lips, your cheek on fire, the red of the one
against the red of the other; lustrous, I'd say;
and always bright, and always florid, and ready
always to escape; your marriage for you
and mine for me, wool, wool, in my face
and cotton in my arms, a linen once I touched
with such a silly reverence, and burlap
with the loose weave, the smell of burlap, and crepe,
the way it draped, the way it absorbed the light;
and lace for romance, and corduroy for romance,
and satin for you, and satin for me, and creases
and buttons, a kind of board, I'd say, a bed,
a cushion for your ear, maybe green, maybe
gray for your hair—and blue for me, or peach—
I love the peach—a scarf for you, a scarf
for me, a white carnation for the cold,
a sunburst, a rose of Sharon for the darkness.

Street of the Butchers

It was called the early years in upstate Pennsylvania
or it was called the first long trek with a footlocker
up over his shoulder so he had to bend both knees
at almost every landing. He held his head
sideways, as if for listening, it was called killing
worms, the bells had already started, the second
or third, he thought; by his calculations, the ringing
would stop by the number seven. He thought maybe
almost two seconds for each long ring; he counted
himself among the chosen ones to be in the
bell's range. He knew he would lie down on his back
after he tried the faucets and opened the windows,
and go to sleep with the sound. It was called
the first concert, the bird in the iron mouth.

Last Home

The name of the alley is Pine Street where the rottweiler
pushed his way into a degrading doghouse
past a filthy towel that served as a floating
door or window to keep out the light. The street
is called Walnut where there is a posted sign
and six or seven refrigerators for sale
in the front yard and two or three boarded-up windows,
and it is Fifth, I think, where I walked through
the mourners in front of the converted synagogue;
and it is one of the hills, Ferry or College,
that I climbed up to see if I could strike a
balance between my leather lung and my sodden
thigh, and which would go first and how long it took
before we could breathe on our own and whether the sycamore
that split the stone sidewalk came by the wind
a half a mile below or it was just planted
for shade and beauty. And how high you had to go
to see both bridges, and where you should stand to hear
the roar, and if you still could hear the ringing.

Larry Levis Visits Easton, PA, During a November Freeze

I said "Dear Larry" as I put down his book, *Elegy*,
across the street from the Home Energy Center

and its two embellished secular Christmas trees
and its two red wreaths over red ribbon crosses

enshrining a thirty-inch stove in one of its windows
and a fifty-gallon water heater in the other,

knowing how wise he would have been with the parking lot
and the tree that refused against all odds and all

sane agreements and codicils to let its dead leaves
for God's sake fall in some kind of trivial decency

and how he would have stopped with me always beside him
to watch a girl in a white fur parka and boots

build the first snowball on Northampton Street she collected
from the hood of a Ford Fairlane underneath that tree

and throw it she thought at a small speed-limit sign
although it landed with a fluff just shy of the twin

painted center lines inducing the three of us,
her lover, Larry, and me to make our own snowballs

from the hoods and fenders of our own Fairlanes although
she threw like none of us and to add to it

she was left-handed, so bless her, may she have
a good job and children and always be free of cancer

and may the two of us scrape some roofs before the
rain relieves us, and may we find gloves for our labor.

Short Words

Some dried-up phlox so old the blue was white
and something like a fireweed and grass
hopeful as always and I with a poison berry
I wanted to eat and make it my morning cracker,
and coffee so sweet I knew I put a sugar
substitute into my cup and milk so sweet
it might have been Carnation, and there was wind,
whether it was the rain coming in or only
a little cleanliness, and in the burn pile
a dead and rusty pine tree halfway sticking
out to remind me of the 1950 Buick
Mike Levey gave me in 1963
and I drove five years later into a junkyard,
and how I lost two jobs and almost three
because I was a little like Amos and longed
only to hear short words and one day a whole
student body waited in the parking lot
while I walked in alone to get my letter
of intent from a nervous college president
with pink fingernails and shaking fingers;
and who was it climbed the six-foot wall by himself
in order to teach his classes the Board of Idiots
at Temple University erected to keep
the Negroes out, and who is still ashamed
after fifty years he turned away from his first
loyalty because someone misspelled a word
or didn't speak French or never had stood with his hand
under his chin supporting the elbow with one
middle finger in front of a gorgeous old
Simone Martini painted on mountain pine;
and this is what Amos taught, that you should rebuke
all liars, straddlers, and accommodators,
all paper rats, all priests with castanets,

and all their scoffing, indifference and silence,
that you should obstruct them and even intervene,
and you should remove the wall and you should grow
your own lilac and you should kiss on the mouth;
dried-out marsh grass, dead lilies, August roses.

Night

If only the bell keeps him alive though that is
an odd way of looking at his new life, then
missing an hour because of sleep or guessing the
time and being off sometimes for two hours
won't be his undoing, not that alone, though it is
hard to attach yourself to a new lover
and learn how she smooths her dress down or listens
to some kind of voice there or to her own silence
which he also listens to hour after hour,
sometimes lying there so long he thinks the cat
has got her tongue or that the electricity
has stopped, as in a flood, though he says to
himself there has to be another system, a
backup generator slow to crank up, he can even
hear the bell slurring, or dragging, a different sound
but reassuring nonetheless, oh more than
that, a gift in his six-hour crisis, a melodic
stroking, it is new to him, and hearing it when
it is dark and he is freezing, though pleasantly,
but lying awake, and guessing, he sometimes gets it
right on the hour, but sometimes night has just started,
the drunks are only coming home and he has
four or five more hours, the sound is brief,
forbidding, harsh, indifferent, and he is surprised that
he has guessed wrong, a voice has wounded him, wind
has slammed his window shut or his door but he
just lies on his back and even opens his eyes
in the dark, for that is a life too, and he turns
to one side or the other and hangs onto something,
a chair, a windowsill, and waits for the next
shocking stroke and sometimes he changes pillows.

Drowning on the Pamet River

Because of the pull I ended up swimming in the grasses
a hundred yards from nowhere my beloveds
ready to jump in after me a black willow
rushing in to save me—my kind of dolphin—you
think I struggled a yard at a time but I was
nudged a little that's why my lips were red
instead of blue that's why I had the words
to "The Dipsy Doodle" still on my tongue and I was
waltzing under your huge white towel your bathrobe
over my head hot tea already burning
my throat that's why I loved the two Labradors
so much that's why I kissed you so desperately.

Mexican

for A.M.M.

By holding the mirror above my head your face
was tilted just enough so that the light
came in between the window and the tree
and half the clouds were shining and by twisting
one way then the other first the rays,
though beaten into the tin, half rose above
the painted bricks as if they came from your eyes
and not the other way around and second
your hair changed color since there was red somewhere
and light was the cause, although there were my wrinkles
and there was my stubble since it was already morning,
but when it came to that, by turning the mirror
a little one way half my face was in shadow
and there was a shadow under the tree, a classic
tree shadow, perfect for robins tearing those
living worms apart—if it was April and
there was some air in the ground; and we were looking
ravenous and whimsical, your right hand
was on my shoulder and we were struggling a little
to hold the mirror straight, for topping it off
there was a vertical on either side and
they were on hinges, we could close them like doors
and cover up the center glass or we could
move them back and forth and get a triple
or even quadruple image, we could grieve
three or four times at once and we could kiss
for hours if we held the doors just so,
and it was a kind of relief that we would miss
the lavender rising over the city—you would
call it purple anyhow, you would fight me
on blues, I know—and it was almost a pleasure
that we would miss the thaw, the river rising

and fog and pneumonia and gardens turning red
in the wrong season and ice melting and mud
wherever we walked and lightning storms without
the sound of thunder as if we were deaf and nights
so warm the phoebes were terrified and titmice
were starting to hunt for grasses while we made love.

Paris

As I recall the meal I ate was liver
with mashed potatoes, and out of simple courtesy
I kept what I could in my briefcase or half hidden
under the table; I think an Underwood brought me
two months' free living and the Polish architect
I sold it to whose teeth the Germans had smashed
at Auschwitz it gave him seven months at least,
depending on other forces. The whole thing
lasted maybe a year for by my reckoning
when I was ready to leave the stores were already
full of new things and they were cleaning the bridges
and polishing the squares. My own time
was somewhere between the Ordeal and the Recovery,
but there was food enough. The one thing
I remember about him we had the same
name in Hebrew though I don't know what he was called
in Polish—I hope not Gerald—we always walked
after lunch and stopped for coffee. By my
reckoning he was in his forties. I went
to Italy on that money, it was my first
grant, a little hopeless by later standards,
but that only made it easier to practice
deprivation—in one or two years—ketchup
with beans, seven pounds of lamb for a dollar,
bread eight cents a loaf. It was
more loyal that way, I was so stubborn I did it
ten years too long, maybe twenty, it was
my only belief, what I went there for.

Already April

The second day in a row I watched the same
untrimmed drooping woody forsythia
for I was thinking of getting ready, though this time
I couldn't find the shirt I wanted or even
one dry chair to sit on though I found
a violet for my hair for I was lucky,
counting the first ten houses south of the creek,
and no one had a stump that huge and yellow
poison frothing like that and white moths drowning
in what they thought was soup, and no one studied
the obituaries like that or scattered petals
when he walked through the geese and calmed them down
by talking to the bowlegged guards and whispering
something from before the war half almost
joyous half ironic given the fact that
it was already April and no one I loved had
died since early November and this year the bush
turned yellow much too soon, it was so hot
so early, I almost felt cheated, the zone I'm in,
north of Trenton and south of Allentown,
I had been so ashamed and outmaneuvered.

March 27

The hat he bought in 1949 for
fifty cents, he knew it for sure, the scarf
in 1950, for fourteen cents, he planted
his beans three inches apart, two inches deep,
and put a worm in every two holes for he was
giving back and for this purpose he carried
a twenty-ounce can without a label though it had
probably housed asparagus tips or even
French-cut beans itself, and that should be coming
full cycle, and he would get on his knees for that and
let the water take him where it had to, he
was where he wanted to be, his shirt cost a quarter,
his pants cost eighty cents, but that was before
the legs were covered with mud; the can was rusty
and both of his hands were red, he was on a hill
down from the cheap mulberry, the birch
was in a corner by itself, his shoulder
was getting tender but he had fifty more worms
to go—or a hundred—he used a stick and he would
stay there at least an hour—swelling or no swelling—
and he would finish his scraping, God or no God.

August 20–21

   In the age of loosestrife
a man walked down then up on the waterway
overwhelmed by the basic weeds in August which
having their last chance they stopped disguising
and flowered one more time he thought though he
may just as well have been thinking of the briefcase,
the first time in six or seven years,
and what it had inside as well as the smoothness
since it was calfskin and a gift from his son
to boot, which broke his heart, and past two small
roses of Sharon, one of the plants which gave him
endless pleasure, ridiculously on the bank of
the waterways as if they somehow were wild,
and weeds to boot, though he knew where they came from and
where the mother was planted, he had walked there so
much and by the color of the flower he
could identify it too exactly the same as
the one up north, exactly the same as the one
behind his outhouse in central Pennsylvania, though
they came in purple too, they must have been planted
to hold the soil down, to give some color, for
now he realized how far what he called the mother was
planted, near some locusts, near an iron fence,
and one of the locusts was eighty feet high, the trunk
was covered with poison ivy almost as far as
the first fork, and on his way back he stopped
by the dusty cornflowers for he was beleaguered and only
blue could help him though they were almost dead,
the way they get, and he was worn out and had to
force himself a little when he got up
from his chair, he found himself rocking for leverage,
it was a kind of joke, and it was funny, the
flag next door, a striped green and brown disc,

and next to that, two houses down, a faded
American, with fifty states, all those who
live near rivers display their flags, it is
the jauntiness, not the patriotism, he has
lost so many things, now he is losing
souls, the *New York Times* keeps track of that,
here is the carrot, here is the snowflake ragweed
he hung on another fork, it is weird that
one day it's in the business section, one day
it's in the Metro, here he is strewing his sage
and here he is strewing his coneflower, there's a daisy
and he doesn't know what it stands for though he strews it
more than he does the others, everyone has
his own water, sore decayer, he stands
above the spillway and he walks back as he did
a thousand times, the pain is in his knee,
he loves the wetness, he hates the violent sneezing.

This Life

for A.M.M.

Mostly I opened my napkin with a flair
and held my two hands neatly in my lap
or tapped the spoon as if I were deep in thought,
and once or twice I worked on a small fish
until the bones were free of almost everything
resembling this life for I was against corruption
of any kind and I ate pears and apples
until I almost exploded, and on my way
to Sarah Lawrence College in early September,
1997, I broke a white cloud in
half, through one of my open windows and watched
it change two times before I was over the bridge,
struggling to see in my mirror, and I would have given
you your half except it was gone in a minute,
just like the phlox I gave you and the rose
that turned to dust when I touched it; mostly I drove
close to the side of the road for I was careful
of all the exits and I turned at the last
second or I would have drifted through God knows what
blocks of pure Spanish with my Italian lips
looking for north and slowing down my guess is
at every corner and breathing a little since water
was gone from my life—or would have been gone—if I hadn't
found my exit, and I could concentrate now
on whether the petals were evenly dispersed
and whether the leaves were shiny or not and what
loves acid and what is hairy and what is lacy
and when it is good for eating and should you drink it
and if it was streaked with green or spotted with purple
and if it was sweet and vernal, the cloud I gave you.

Snowdrop

There had to be more than one day of rain
and temperatures in the fifties, but even more
there had to be a letup for us to go out
with one umbrella between the four of us
and give up our argument for a minute
for one of us even to notice; and since she
came from one zone north of us and there was
a catch in her voice when she bent down we stopped
short in the rain to see the green unlacing
the white, of all places in zone six,
where half our ideas come from and umbrellas
are used with a vengeance; though as I remember
it was more like a cry and so loving that
I was a little jealous, and when she touched me,
and her way is a hand on the back, loverly
the way she gets, I coughed for comfort and even
the purple stones were a comfort, the way they bulge
like buttresses, and since the mournful Chow,
of all the dogs that ruined our walk, only stared
and if he barked it was almost silent we had
time in between to look at the white sycamores
and balance wood with water and hate umbrellas.

Last Blue

You want to get the color blue right,
just drink some blue milk from a blue cup;
wait for the blue light of morning
or evening with its blue aftermath.

You want to understand,
look at the parking lines outside my window,
the neon moon outside Jabberwocky's.

And funk! You have to know funk.
A touch of blue at the base of the spine;
long threads going into your heart;
a steaming fountain you pour into your own bowl.

My dead sister's eyes!
Those of her porcelain twin at the Lambertville Flea,
twenty dollars a day for the small table,
all the merde you need to get you across the river.

And one kind of blue for a robin's egg;
and one kind of blue for a bottle of ink.
Two minds to fathom the difference.

Your earrings which as far as I can see
are there as much to play with as to look at.
Your blue pencil
which makes your eyes Egyptian. Bluebells, bluebirds,

from Austin, Texas, the dead hackster
who drank potassium, Governor Bush
who drank milk of magnesia; a chorus of saints
from Wylie Avenue and one kind of blue

for my first prayer shawl and one kind of blue for the robe
Fra Lippo gave to Mary. Blue from Mexico
and blue from Greece, that's where the difference lay
between them, in the blues; a roomful of scholars,

in Montreal one year, in New York another,
that is blue, blue was their speech, blue
were their male and female neckties, their food was blue,
their cars were rented, Christmas lights

were in the lobby, one of the bars had peanuts
in all the urns and on the upper floors
the hospitality rooms were crowded with livid
sapphire cobalt faces—I was blue

going into the tunnel, I am blue every night
at three or four o'clock; our herring was blue,
we ate it with Russian rye and boiled potatoes,
and in the summer fresh tomatoes, and coffee

mixed with sugar and milk; I sat in a chair
so close to Sonny Terry I could hear
him mumble, the criticism he made
of his own sorrow, but I was that close to Pablo

Casals in 1950, talk about blue, and
though I left it a thousand times I stood—
since I didn't have a seat—in front of an open
window of Beth Israel in Philadelphia

to hear the sobbing, such a voice, a dog
came up to me that night out of the blue
and put his muzzle in my hand nor would he
leave me for a minute, he would have stayed

———————

with me forever and followed me up to my house
which butted onto the woods in back of the synagogue
and sat outside my door; or blue on the street
outside a Parlour near the Port Authority—

my seed inside—or blue in Ocean Grove
where sky and sea combined and walking the boardwalk
into the wind and blue in a shrink's small parking lot
watching the clock and blue in my mother's arms

always comforting her and blue with my daughter
starving herself and blue with my wife all day
playing solitaire or drawing houses and blue,
though smiling, when I came into the world, they called me

Jess Willard, thirteen pounds, and I had just hammered
Jack Dempsey into the ropes and I was shouting—
in a tinny voice—it sounded like someone weeping—
it always sounded like that— everything living.

Kingdom

As far as the color red
there was a splash in the southeast corner where
the tree I adored was dying.

And as for blue
it lay between the door and the first dogwood
sprawled and sucked and wilted.

And there was a definite tilt to the new apartment house
with pots of iris on the roof
and there was an indentation where a false
Italian had laid the bricks, the line was crooked
and once he got started nothing could stop him, seventy
bricks an hour, seven hundred a day.

As for daisies, I compare them to dogs
because of the commonality, I almost
want to say the loving community
as in the parks in downtown Philadelphia,
Mario Lanzo for one, Judy Garland another.

And as for the watering can,
and as for the ginkgo with its transitional leaf,
and as for the snapdragons, oh
I will sit and wait for that and I will
bend to pick them one by one, the red,
the orange, the mixed; and as for the railroad bridge
how long it will last,
and as for the rope hanging down from a girder, the weighted
ball a foot above the water, the life
in the river almost clearer with its simple
obscurities and new arrangements, the bushes
where they belong, inside the girders, a stray

Canada goose to swim above the cloud-stream;
and as for the bike path, how we passed each other
hugging the wall and riding on the edge,
and where we ended, either the road in front of
the billboard or the steep steps cut at an angle
below the greasy fireplace, there was—
as far as I can tell—a breaking point
and one path down and one path up,
for it was a kind of park
with grass and chains and benches
and little walkways
and fish inside a window
swimming from river to river
and I began to shiver
over my *New York Times.*

As for our touching foreheads,
and as for dancing with you and knocking books
and candlesticks on the floor,
and then our talk on Jesus, as for whether
he had a sister and whether he limped and whether he
disappeared, see Luke, and more and more
dancing, as far as that; and as for the kingdom
and what it meant in my life, how it was
sometimes like a cloud, how I used to stand
on the sidewalk and put my hand on the wall, I had
such pleasure I never wanted to move, the world
around me stopped, I think, and how I later
made my own kingdom, but I was fourteen or fifteen,
and how it wasn't what Auden thought, mere drabbles of
Sunday school Isaiah and magazine Marx but
something sweeter than that and not just bony
justice and stringy wealth, say something out of the
letters we had in the thirties, WPA,
with a vengeance, nor was it kingdom come,
dying will be done, and though it would always

be later and later I loved it just as it was,
and I could smell it, it was hidden in the coal
and in the snow and in the noise the streetcars
made rounding the bend and picking up speed, I loved
walking all morning in the snow, I climbed
up icy steps thinking of how could beasts
lie down together and could the corruptible
just vanish like that, for it was a difficult climb,

and as for us, nothing was broken, only
a wine glass maybe, or an earring was lost—

and as for that, I would have broken a dish
or thrown my favorite teapot on the floor
or smashed the red and white rooster with the candy corn
feet and caramelized comb, although I would have
caressed him first since he guarded my house
and sang in an amorous voice, as far as that.

from
American Sonnets

Winter Thirst

I grew up with bituminous in my mouth
and sulfur smelling like rotten eggs and I
first started to cough because my lungs were like cardboard;
and what we called snow was gray with black flecks
that were like glue when it came to snowballs and made
them hard and crusty, though we still ate the snow
anyhow, and as for filth, well, start with
smoke, I carried it with me I know everywhere
and someone sitting beside me in New York or Paris
would know where I came from, we would go in for dinner—
red meat loaf or brown *choucroute*—and he would
guess my hill, and we would talk about soot
and what a dirty neck was like and how
the white collar made a fine line;
and I told him how we pulled heavy wagons
and loaded boxcars every day from five
to one a.m. and how good it was walking
empty-handed to the No. 69 streetcar
and how I dreamed of my bath and how the water
was black and soapy then and what the void
was like and how a candle instructed me.

June

Since it is June already I could be back there
wearing a yellow hat to confuse the blue jay
or giving in to the smells; and once the heat
lets up I could be shivering in a T-shirt,
wishing I had a wool sweater, remembering
the bricks in this room and how we hated plaster
yet how we painted them white and how advanced
we felt when we finally had a telephone;
and I could be picking phlox by pulling the low-lying
roots and stop to think if there could be pomp
enough with only a single four-pointed star;
and I could bend down again for the chicory
that sky and land conspired so much with it caught
the sun for a minute, and put it over my sink,
the way we brought something into the house
that we could cut the dead leaves from and water,
now that we had a well, now that the wind
was breaking down the door and one of the old
zinc pennies was standing on end and we could find
the key inside the crock, now we had light.

Aberdeen Proving Grounds, 1946

I have had the honor of being imprisoned, the
joy of breaking stone with a sledgehammer, the
pleasure of sleeping under a bare lightbulb, the
grief of shitting with a guard watching, the
sorrow of eating by myself, and I have
felt the lightness of being released and watched the
leaves change color from a speeding car,
and I first read the Gospels then, a stiff
and swollen paperback, the way paper
was made then, and I slept peacefully,
a blanket over the steel, as I recall,
though I planned the same murder every night,
which kept me going my thirteen working hours;
and when I got home I threw my duffel bag into
the river and walked to the No. 69 streetcar,
and even the clothes I wore, even the shoes,
even the overcoat, I stuffed into
the hot incinerator and listened to the roar
three stories down and watched the particles float
inside the chute and read an old newspaper
on top of the bundle and tested the cord and cleaned
the greasy window, since I was cleaning everything.

For the Bee

The fence itself can't breathe, jewelweeds are choking
the life out of the dirt, not one tomato plant
can even survive, the crows are leaving, the worms
themselves won't stay, the bricks are hot, the water
in one of my buckets has disappeared, and I
am trying to get a pencil out of my pocket
without breaking the point though it is painful
turning sideways in this heat and lifting my
leg like that; and there is a half-dead bee
drowning in my saucer and there is a dirty
kitchen window in which I sit in front of
a piece of rough slate and hold my book to the light
like someone under a tree and nod with tears
of mercy—for the bee I guess—and stare
and frown by turns and turn my head to the tree
so I can be kind and let the filtered light
go in and out and wave a little because of the
glass the way I do when I am facing
myself in the mirror and not even ridicule
the new president and not even loathe him.

Alone

I was alone and I could do what I wanted—
I couldn't believe my luck—if I wanted to sleep
at ten in the morning I could sleep or two
in the afternoon, if that was my time, or wander
by car or foot delicately in the night
when everything was resting exhausted and stop to
eat in quiet, no humor at last, oh coffee,
coffee, I was sitting alone at a counter—
I was in a painting sort of—closeness
closer than love between me and the waitress,
and when I paid the bill more closeness; I walked
from window to window, once I walked the length
of Amsterdam Avenue, once I walked from Lake
Garda to Venice, a hundred miles, and Venice
south to Florence, through Bologna; I ate
mortadella cheap I washed in the fountains
I slept with the barking dogs and twice in my life
I woke up surrounded, once on the floor of a train station,
once on the floor of a bank. I left at five
or six in the morning; I put my keys in a bottle;
I wore two pair of socks and hid my money.

September, 1999

I was thinking about pears—or you were—I
don't remember who first started to think,
though you said Seckel pears and I said Bartlett
and nothing I could do could budge you; I
could cut the skin so quickly and keep it so thin
the light goes through it, and I held it to the light
to catch the rose, and I knew when the core was
already brown and it was spreading just by
touching the flesh, and sometimes the neck was gone,
as far as eating, though you would call it the nose,
you with your Seckels, you with your freckles, and no one
but me has quite such pleasure extruding the stem,
and no one I know puts a pear in his coat pocket
when he goes out in the rain, as I do, though what
was the pleasure eating in sheets of water compared to
the loneliness eating by yourself, and even though
hornets were in your bowl and ten or twenty
were crawling over a rotten peach and three or
four were already after my pear since it was
autumn again and hornets were dying and they were
angry, and drunk, I just wiped them away.

You

You know my story better than I do and if
I stray a little you will correct me but more
like a child corrects his mother, entwined as they are,
when even a word is mispronounced or some
small detail is passed over, especially
how many teeth were in a mouth or what
the name of the wolf was—or the green spider—
only for once it is smells we are talking about
and I am trying to describe a fragrance
by using words and I try desperately
to do it, and you nod by way of agreement,
knowing how difficult and even ridiculous
it is and we both know that only by likeness
can we be near, comparison I should say,
and both of us struggle to describe the smell of
snow in 1940, mixed as it was with
coal fumes and the rawness of locusts in that
foggy mountain climate and an air
explosive with dust and dirt from the steel mills rising
like orange fat for the gods, though you weren't born yet.

The Ink Spots

The thing about the dove was how he cried in
my pocket and stuck his nose out just enough to
breathe some air and get some snow in his eye and
he would have snuggled in but I was afraid
and brought him into the house so he could shit on
the *New York Times*, still I had to kiss him
after a minute, I put my lips to his beak
and he knew what he was doing, he stretched his neck
and touched me with his open mouth, lifting
his wings a little and readjusting his legs,
loving his own prettiness, and I just
sang from one of my stupid songs from one of my
vile decades, the way I do, I have to
admit it was something from *trains*. I knew he'd like that,
resting in the coal car, slightly dusted with
mountain snow, somewhere near Altoona,
the horseshoe curve he knew so well, his own
moan matching the train's, a radio
playing the Ink Spots, the engineer roaring.

Exordium and Terminus

In your rendition of *The Year 25–25*
the airplane rattles, the engine roars, the sardines
around me smile, like sardines, and you kiss me
twice, once on the cheek and once on the ear.
It is a song from 1965–1970;
some keeper of music will know the title, the singer,
where it was on the charts, what it reflects
of what was Doomsday then and how long it stayed
in the top ten or twenty. And who was president,
whether he had a girlfriend, whether J. Edgar
was still around and whether or not his boyfriend
ate cottage cheese like him. And what I was doing,
and what car I was driving, and how much money I
owed to banks, universities and relatives.
And whether *I* had a girlfriend and what her breasts
were like—and her mind—and did I like being
subversive, and who would sleep with Nixon? and what was
the name of the motel on Route 22 that cost
twenty dollars in 1973, and was it
wrong to prefer the Watergate hearings to making
love, and how the pigs have taken over Doomsday.

In Time

As far as clocks—and it is time to think of them—
I have one on my kitchen shelf and it is
flat, with a machine-made flair, a perfect
machine from 1948, at the latest,
and made of shining plastic with the numbers
sharp and clear and slightly magnified in
that heartbreaking postwar style, the cord
too short, though what does it matter, since the mechanism
is broken and it sits unplugged alongside a
cheap ceramic rooster, his head insanely
small and yet his tiny brain alert for
he is the one who will crow and not that broken
buzzing relic, though time is different now
and dawn is different too, you were up all night
and it is dark when he crows and you are waiting
to see what direction you should face and if
you were born in time or was it wasted and what
the day looks like and is the rooster loyal.

Les Neiges d'Antan

Where art thou now, thou Ruth whose husband in the snow
creased thy head with a tire iron, thou who wore
ridiculous hats when they were the rage and loved
exotic cultures and dances such as the *Haitian
Fling* and the *Portuguese Locomotive*, my wife
hated because of her snooty attitude
or that her hair was swept up and her nose was aquiline
and her two boys raised hell with our green apples
the Sunday they came to visit, she in whose Mercury
we parked for over a year, every night
in front of her mother's house in one of the slightly
genteel streets that led into the park
the other side downhill really from the merry-go-round,
or where is Nancy or who is the Nancy Ezra Pound
located in between his racial diatribes
and dry lyrics three times at least in the *Cantos*,
but tell me where that snow is now and tell me—
as in *where is Tangerine* and *where is Flora*—
how old Ruth is and where does she live and does she
still dance the *Locomotive* and does she bundle.

Hydrangea

I was pleased by blue hydrangea because at
last I had a flower from a gorgeous .
family I could hate just as when certain
say Jewish poets, whom I'm supposed to revere
because they're Jewish and not to love them would be
an act of betrayal to all eleven prophets;
dozens of kings and clothing manufacturers;
dentists, chess players, swimmers, stockbrokers, English teachers;
psychiatrists, painters, physicists, salesmen, violinists;
social workers, merchants, lawyers, cutters, trimmers;
critics; reveal themselves as snobs and bigots
and analytical and anti-passionate which could be
for all I know another side of Judaism
since Judaism has three sides as in the
Mercy, as in the Exceptions, as in the Melancholies,
which takes me back to the blue hydrangea I see
between an opening in the fence, it looks like
the blue was painted on, I hate it, I also
hate the red carnation, I love the cream
and when it's cone-shaped, I even like the pink,
may God forgive me, Lord of the lost and destitute.

Spider

How you like these threads, said white spider
traveling back and forth between two rooms in
Lambertville, New Jersey, his web a work of
art, truly excessive, spit from his soul,
and the first case of any spit, it came from
my own soul since I am a mimic neurotic.
But how you like my steel? You like my window?
You like my big eye waiting? How you like my
chandelier? How you like fate? You like
my silk? Do cover your legs, do tighten
the arms a little, do tighten around the neck.
And how you like my kiss? How about
my rasping bloody tongue? Weren't those herbs
and such like any household, giant unkempt
Russian sage, the better to smell you, my dear,
and spicy rosemary beside the orange and
purple echinacea, all that a little
to placate—though I know you don't believe it,
for nature is nature—your perverted Isaiah
from running around like crazy in the meat markets.

Iris

The lock was on the right although I had to
open it from the left so I could use
my other hand to turn the knob and there were
four windows facing the street and for a
study I put my feet on the painted board
that covered the radiator and that's where I
slept for an hour since it was too exhausting
to cross the room, and when I got up I walked
downstairs so I could sit in the square on one
of the cold benches behind the limp flags
for it was two in the morning and the prostitutes
were making faces at the slow-moving cop cars
and smoking cigarettes the secondhand smoke of
which I moved two benches away to escape
though I didn't say a word nor did they ask me
for anything more than a cigarette, and one of them
gave me a flower, it was a faded blue iris,
and it was cold that night, I put it inside
my shirt so I could hurry home to adore it.

Grand Hotel

The time I took Anne Marie to what had been
a Nazi brothel in Prague some tourists were standing
under the chandelier and some leftover communist
stood there explaining the thickness of glass and what
the history was of glassmaking in the Czech
Republic, and we walked through them to get
seats so we could suck in the *Art Nouveau*
over our coffee and undercooked pancakes
before we got into the ancient elevator
and went back to our room, *en suite*, as it were,
and dirty, dark, and seedy at that, and looked
in the bottom of the wardrobe, behind the blankets,
to see what they did with love—the pricks—and could
we sleep on that mattress, and how thick was the window glass,
and this time walked down the great marble staircase
holding hands the whole way down, nor did I
bark even once or say *fuck you* to the Germans.

Sam and Morris

I had two uncles who were proletarians
and one of them was a housepainter and one of them
was a carpenter—they beat their wives
regularly and they had nineteen children
between them. Once a month or so my father
would go to one of their houses to intervene
and once I remember a police car with a dog.
When I was home on a short furlough I went
with my mother and father to a Jewish restaurant
and there, sitting in the back, were my two uncles,
in their seventies by then, and eating together,
chicken, chopped liver, God knows what, but pickles
and coleslaw, there always were pickles and coleslaw
and they were almost conspiring, it seemed to me
then, so young I was, and I was reading my
Ezra Pound already and I was ashamed of
what he said about Jews. Of usury those
two unshaven *yidden*, one of them red-eyed
already from whiskey, they knew nothing, they never
heard of Rothschild. Their hands were huge and stiff,
they hardly could eat their *kreplach*, Pound, you bastard!

Burning

Where is the mind that asked whether the drugstore
that stood at the crest of a hill and had a beacon
as its emblem, and I ate fruit salad sundaes there
and grilled cheese sandwiches, was or wasn't a tower,
in the sense that there were porches, windows and staircases,
in the sense that there were mirrors and shining lamps
and one or two banners, and what was a tower doing there
with me walking to the library and post office,
and only a Chinese restaurant next door;
and where is the mind that abided the large plaza
outside the drugstore and made its own canopies
and beautiful flying objects, and where did the tower
come from and the dream of emptiness
that has abided for more than fifty years,
and the heart which burned, such was burning, and such
was the tower, it also burned, only in that case
it wasn't attached to anything, it burned
of its own volition and mountains in Pennsylvania
still burn, alas, they have an abode, and empty
bottles explode and paper flutes burn and birdsong.

Studebaker

Try a small black radio from any year
and listen to the voices you get, they were
much faster then, they raced ahead of us
and rushed the music; love was in a rocking chair,
the floor was crooked, the moon was already in
the sky, though it was daylight still; or love
was in a Studebaker, we were driving east
and we had no idea how long the corporation
would last, or if there was a corporation, how could we?
And did it have its headquarters in Delaware
for taxes and connections, though the doors
were heavy and solid, what was the year? '55?
The Lark appeared in 1958 or
'59—it was their last attempt,
though I remember the Wagoneer, it was 19-
66 and something called the Cruiser, we had
Nat King Cole on the radio though static
was bad in Pennsylvania, given the mountains,
and there was a lever you pushed to make a bed—
I hope I'm getting it right—the leaves on the windshield
were large and wet, the song was "Unforgettable,"
the tree was either a swamp maple or a sycamore.

Cost

From the beginning it was the money, how I
could live on seven dollars a week anywhere
outside the U.S. or go to France
on the G.I. Bill, and learn to love cauliflower.
Although the Caribbean was even cheaper
and Mexico cheaper than that. You wouldn't believe
what life was like after the war, that was
the time, if ever, to live on nothing. I was
enflamed by an article in *Look* magazine,
news went sideways then, but I had already
spent a year in New York City. I was
more or less getting ready, and it was odd
that money would so engross me; I got started
early and it went on for years; I kept
notebooks then as I do now; I love
looking at the stacks of figures, how much
it cost to read Catullus in Latin, what it
cost to understand Villon, including
the price of books and bicycles, not to mention
the price of a lost epic—by week or by month—
and what my ignorance cost and what my stubbornness.

Still Burning

Me trying to understand say whence
say whither, say what, say me with a pencil walking,
say reading the dictionary, say learning medieval
Latin, reading Spengler, reading Whitehead,
William James I loved him, swimming breaststroke
and thinking for an hour, how did I get here?
Or thinking in line, say the 69 streetcar
or 68 or 67 Swissvale,
that would take me elsewhere, me with a textbook
reading the pre-Socratics, so badly written,
whoever the author was, me on the floor of
the lighted stacks and sitting cross-legged,
walking afterwards through the park or sometimes
running across the bridges and up the hills,
sitting down in our tiny dining room,
burning in a certain way, still burning.

Roses

There was a rose called Guy de Maupassant,
a carmine pink that smelled like a Granny Smith
and there was another from the seventeenth century
that wept too much and wilted when you looked;
and one that caused tuberculosis, doctors
dug them up, they wore white masks and posted
warnings in the windows. One wet day
it started to hail and pellets the size of snowballs
fell on the roses. It's hard for me to look at
a Duchess of Windsor, it was worn by Franco
and Mussolini, it stabbed Jews; yesterday I bought
six roses from a Haitian on Lower Broadway;
he wrapped them in blue tissue paper, it was
starting to snow and both of us had on the wrong shoes,
though it was wind, he said, not snow that ruined
roses and all you had to do was hold them
against your chest. He had a ring on his pinky
the size of a grape and half his teeth were gone.
So I loved him and spoke to him in false Creole
for which he hugged me and enveloped me
in his camel hair coat with most of the buttons missing,
and we were brothers for life, we swore it in French.

Hearts

The larger our hearts were, the more
blurred our love was, the softer
our arrows became, the vaguer
our initials, the deeper
the woods were and more abandoned
the more distant we were and more
absurdly hooked by those arrows
and linked by those bulging valves
whose soft contours were widened
with time and roughened at the edges
whatever you were, whatever
the life was that kept us connected,
buried in a birch too close
for comfort to a black locust
whose one side was destroyed
more than half a century
after we stopped downstream
to look at the stone farmhouse,
a fence holding up a dead
rosebush, another birch
starting to sprout, some clattering
and croaking in both directions.

Slash of Red

It was another one of his petite visions
and he had one every day now—at Optiques,
at Gold and Silver—and he ended up,
for it was hard work, sitting against a wall;
and when he looked at the yard he knew the dimensions
were ancient, *holy* he called them, and made comparisons
to African and Turkish rectangles,
only his yard was bare, there were two trees,
and a brick walk going from the gate to the steps.
He said it was Zen-like, only he meant he resisted
the fountaineers and their computer drawings;
it was a straight line, there wasn't a curve
in the middle, there wasn't a jog at the end,
considering that he never used a string,
and he was proud that he had only a trowel
and a little sand to place the bricks. He counted
320, some broken, some not,
and thought about it as a slash of red
against a background of green. This is how
he entered the twenty-first century. More charitable now.

Box of Cigars

I tried either one or two but they were stale
and broke like sticks or crumbled when I rolled them
and lighting a match was useless nor could I
put them back in the refrigerator—
it was too late for that—even licking them
filled my mouth with ground-up outer leaf,
product of Lancaster or eastern Virginia,
so schooled I am with cigars, it comes in the blood,
and I threw handfuls of them into the street
from three floors up and, to my horror, sitting
on my stoop were four or five street people
who ran to catch them as if they were suddenly rich,
and I apologize for that, no one should
be degraded that way, my hands were crazy,
and I ran down to explain but they were smoking
already nor did I have anything to give them
since we were living on beans ourselves, I sat
and smoked too, and once in a while we looked
up at the open window, and one of us spit
into his empty can. We were visionaries.

Justice

Only, to hear him scream, you had to know
that he was in the body of the worm
and even the robin could hear the scream, so close
she was to the shaking ground, and though the struggle
was over in less than a minute, the sun turned red,
as you could see between the birches, but that
was just a decoration, a brief statement
as on a gravestone, *Here lies such and such,*
and at the bottom, below a lily, *the worm*
will lie down with the robin, or it was
two carved roses intertwined, or maybe
the sun was more pink, more from shame, it only
lasted a few seconds considering the
size of things, and more and more the hopping
and screaming, whatever he was, however he was
dismembered, and as for justice, it was redder
still, you would say carmine, you would say ruby,
my clothes were red, my neck and face were scarlet.

American Heaven

A saltwater pond in the Hamptons near David
Ignatow's house, the water up to my chest,
an American Heaven, a dog on the shore, this time
his mouth closed, his body alert, his ears
up, a dog *belongs* in heaven, at least our
kind. An egret skidding to a stop, I'm sure
water snakes and turtles, grasses and weeds,
and close to the water sycamores and locusts,
and pitch pine on the hill and sand in the distance,
and girls could suckle their babies standing in water,
so that was our place of origin, that was
the theory in 1982—David
had his own larder, Rose had hers, he brought
tuna fish into her kitchen, it was a triptych,
the centerpiece was the pond, the left panel
was his, his study, and he was stepping naked
across the frame into the pond holding an
open can and hers was the right, her arms had
entered the pond, holding a bowl, it was her
studio, we ate on a dry stone
and talked about James Wright and Stanley Kunitz,
and there was a star of the fourth magnitude
surrounded by planets, shining on all of us.

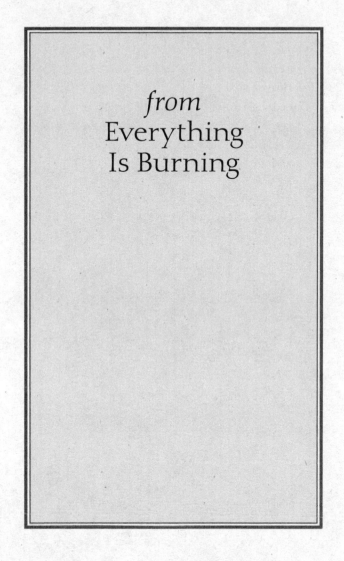

from
Everything
Is Burning

La Pergola

Finally daisies and tomatoes, I have settled for
that and bushes more important than fruit and
flowers and one gray squirrel running back and forth on
the fence and leaping onto the humbled sunflower,
how deep it bows, the tomatoes are only green
and as we speak I am out there bending over,
making a bouquet of daisies, you can
count them, I have five fedoras, there in
the back room of La Pergola I take a
break from eating kasha and varnishkes
to primp and glow, damn the bushes, damn
the bald daisies, stinking blue vase, stinking Dixie cup.

E.P. 1

Nothing matters but the quality of the affection,
neither the bicyclist riding by in her black baseball cap
nor the three trees I planted in my backyard,
I should say four counting the small apple
nailed to my neighbor's fence, nor can I
discount the memory he had of Ferdie and Fordie,
prick and snob though he was. But I never trusted his
paradise, it was too literary, nor his
final confession, nor what he said to Ginsberg—
imagine, imagine—nor, ah, the endless self-pity
taking the place of character, so un-Kung
after all, although there were two paradises,
weren't there, lying master that he was, and
one was a shut garden of pear trees, dancing Nancy.

Albatross 1

Please listen, there's a thing back there I killed
that's spiritual and has two wings like anything
we love forever—take the pigeon, take the
bluebird—I would rather walk with a cane
than hurt a bluebird; I would kill anyone who stuffed
a full-grown frog into a mason jar
and threw him from a third-floor window, the glass
cutting his body, penetrating his mouth
and eyes. You have to get down there and kill
the frog yourself before you run upstairs
and beat him, holding him half out the window, let his
name be erased for the thing back there.

Never Went to Birdland

Never went to Birdland, so what, went to the Y,
danced all night for a quarter, girls sat down
on bridge chairs, can't remember if they were smoking,
men wore jackets and ties, I know the name of
one, I'll call her Doris—that was her name—
her grandfather was a rabbi from Bialystok
and over ninety—she was twenty, I was
twenty-one, I guess, he had to be born
before the Crimean War; and who were the gangs
that built the wide-gauge railroad tracks that reached
the Urals in 1860? He was only
five feet tall, his hands you can't imagine
nor what the sofa was like and what our struggle was.

The Snow on the River

Snow on the river is my guess though any
change in temperature would do and sometimes
filth alone and as for the cracking, that comes
now in March and sometimes even earlier,
one cloud bumping into another as
we used to say, two sticks curling, then exploding,
some seamy actor from the fifties mixing
one smoke with another, his gum popping.

Sylvia

Across a space peopled with stars I am
laughing while my sides ache for existence
it turns out is profound though the profound
because of time it turns out is an illusion
and all of this is infinitely improbable
given the space, for which I gratefully lie
in three feet of snow making a shallow grave
I would have called an angel otherwise and
think of my own rapturous escape from
living only as dust and dirt, little sister.

Hemingway's House

I don't want to go to Hemingway's house,
let him come to mine, walk in and we'll do
The Killers at my kitchen table, he with his
back to the Japanese maple, me with my back
to the Maytag, ginger ale for one, white rum
the other; the dragon and the mayfly,
death and the knowledge of death,
Monk and Bartók all the same to me.

May 30

I had to sit on the steel railroad tracks
to eat my sandwich and you understand I wrapped it
in wax paper since that is as far as I went
in preservation and I remember my serial number
and I was an H in case somebody murdered me
for that was the day we fanned out in all directions
with poppies in one hand and quarters in the other,
the photograph that of a corporal with his balls blown off.

May Frick Be Damned

In Pittsburgh we used to say, "Tomorrow we strike,
go home, make babies," but always with a Polish
accent and the bars were crowded at ten
in the morning. I for one was stopped once
walking on an empty street downtown
with no reason for being there—I had
three dollars in my pocket so I wasn't
guilty of loitering—may Frick be damned
in Hell forever and ever; may money be stuffed
in all his pockets, may an immigrant
set fire to the money; let Wimpy reign,
"Let's you and him kiss," let love take place
in old cars, let them line up at the curb
in Lovers' Lane and let the voyeurs go
from car to car with flashlights, I whisper this.

The Trent Lott, the McNamara Blues

I would be happy if one of them would offer his
finger or a piece of his cock and not the usual
sensitive skin by way of remorse and he could
lick the ground while he does it, either one could
go first, it doesn't matter, one could sing his
"We Shall Overcome," the other could do his
"Let's Remember Pearl Harbor" but he has to
include the introduction which on hearing
in Woolworth's over and over sitting down
at the Whites Only section in 1941
I memorized but all involuntarily,
or they could lop their arms off as the saints
of Christ did when they lost Jerusalem on
the boats going back to France and tossed them overboard;
and there is a basket just for remorseful limbs
in front of the Library hard by the bored lions
only half a block from W. W. Norton my
publisher I could walk to and sing
for this is what singers are for, little darling.

The Tie

for MARK HILLRINGHOUSE

The other time I wore a tie my friend Mark
had called me that Berrigan had died
and there was a funeral at St. Mark's
and Kenneth Koch and John Ashbery were speaking
on his behalf to those who guard the mountain
and though it was a hundred degrees I stopped in
a Goodwill to buy the tie and a jacket as well
which made me look like a priest or a head
waiter at a French restaurant in the upper Fifties,
the tie alone gave such a look of dignity
and even stiffened my neck when it came to lowlife
poets and painters, dozens of whom were there
filling up the pews; and there was a painting by
Alice Neel of Berrigan in an armchair
facing the pews and afterwards we walked, even
sort of marched down Second Avenue to the apartment,
someone in front holding the painting up,
only Berrigan was naked and the fat rolled
over the edge of the armchair and Alice—Alice
Notley—was sitting in the back bedroom
to escape the praises and afterwards Mark and I
walked back to my car and on the way I threw
the tie and jacket into a large wire basket,
my short-sleeved shirt was soaked and we told stories
about his life in the Polish and Ukrainian marshes.

Boléro

So one day when the azalea bush was firing
away and the Japanese maple was roaring I
came into the kitchen full of daylight and
turned on my son's Sony sliding over the
lacquered floor in my stocking feet for it was
time to rattle the canisters and see what
sugar and barley have come to and how *Boléro*
sounds after all these years and if I'm loyal
still and when did I have a waist that thin?
And if my style was too nostalgic and where
were you when I was burning alive, nightingale?

Stern Country

For sleeplessness, your head facedown, your shoulder blades
floating and aspirin as a last resort, when
death is threatening, though lately I have experimented
with numbers and as for dreams I've never been boring
and only once did I bite the arm of a woman
sitting next to me and I should be careful,
she might have a handwritten poem or a memoir
and didn't I bite her arm and aren't we both
poets, though I warn her that I make gurgling
noises and twitch in both legs and make the bed
jump and I am exhausted from looking at poems
and I don't care about her nuts and bolts
and she has to go to the wilderness herself
and fuck the exercises, let her get smashed
by a Mack truck, then she'll be ready to mourn.

Gimbel's

For only three dollars I was able to see
D. H. Lawrence's dirty pictures which
Scotland Yard in its artistic wisdom
let him take to New Mexico provided
he kept them there, something like that, and he was
ordered not to come back to England with a
hard-on or he would face constabulatory wrath
and he was ordered not to piss on concrete
or even the grass that grows between the cracks
but find a splintered telephone pole or a wall
and share his business there with dogs since he
himself was more an animal than a man,
he says so himself, and love belongs in the coal cellar,
I myself have proof of this; I fantasized
when I was thirty or so that the beds at Gimbel's
the rows and rows of them, the tufted, the striped
one morning a week, not to interrupt sales,
not to make anyone nervous, or walk with her head down
or hold her hand on her mouth, would be given over
to public fucking, I would have been so happy.

Lilies

Those lilies of the field, one Sunday night
I got caught in Pocono traffic and sat there
for twenty minutes during the which in front
a madman saw me in his mirror and leaped
out of his car and running screamed Dr. Stern
I followed your advice I gave up everything
Thoreau was right simplicity I was your
student the which I stared at him the cars were
starting up again but I no longer
believed and had to leave him stranded, I
love you, I shouted, read something else, I would
have pulled off the side of the road but there was no
shoulder there and so I lost him, whatever his
name was. I made a sharp left turn and that was
that, but what I owe him in his under
shirt, how long his beard was then, his eyes
were blue, his tires were bald, what Christ owes me!

Loyal Carp

I myself a bottom-feeder I knew what
a chanson à la carp was I a lover
of carp music for I heard carp singing
behind the glass on the Delaware River,
keeping the shad themselves company
and always it was a basso, in that range there
was space for a song compleat, it was profundo
enough and just to stop and drink in that
melody and just to hum behind those
whiskers, that was muck enough for my life.

Golden Rule

All she wants is for you to stay away from her egg
and all she wants is for you to shut up when it comes
to the three things she hates the most: justice,
mercy, humility. She detests Jesus and she can define
what he is, and was, and wants to be while flying
unbearably low by the one word, "squawk"; and
that is why I pulled my straw hat down over
my bald head and that is why my orange cat
almost died with fear and why she won
the argument with her big black shadow while resting only on one leg.

L'Chaim

There goes that toast again, four chipped
glasses full of some kind of ruby held up
to the sun this time, death crumbs falling and rising
like dust-motes, fish eggs, bubbles, here's to you, bubbles,
here's to Mardi Gras, here's to the apple tree
pinned against my fence, here's to reproach,
here's to doing it to music, here's to fog,
and here's to fog again, and life dividing
inside the fog; oh when it dissipates
let's make a circle; here's to the baby hiding
inside his clothes, here's to his being
alive without me, here's to the mountain again,
for what the hell, I might as well be on the mountain,
here's to delectables, free health care, love, popcorn.

Cigars

The same cracked hoarse nasal sexy laugh—
I almost lifted my face out of the newspaper
to remind her of the drowned bee and the shaky
pedestrian bridge, I almost told her her
favorite passage of Mahler, we were that close
going up and down the ladders and interchanging
souls with each other, we were that overlapping,
appearing and disappearing, that prayerful,
lighting each other's cigars inside the room of laurel-green horse laughter.

Shouldering

We were surrounded by buttercup and phlox
so you know what the month was, one of us had
Sarah Vaughan in her inner ear, one of us
Monk, who put a table there we didn't
know but we were more or less grateful nor was it
even chained to anything and the eggs we
ate were perfect, I cracked them on my head
as I always do and shattered them with my fist,
the grape tomatoes which only cost a dollar
a pint were almost acid-free, the tire
was growing softer but I was a veteran
of *real* tires, and bumper jacks, I even go
back to steaming radiators, I could
tell you things, I said to Monk, I walked
two miles once with a half-gallon of gas
leaking out of an orange juice carton, "In My
Solitude" he said, "September Song," said she.

Bejewels

It were the ink splats from a writing machine
I bought so many centuries ago I
hardly could lift it down from the luggage rack
along with my socks and such, for while the others
converted to Braille I stuck with the splats, I didn't
even do *la touche*, the period in between that
lasted thirty years, I stuck with splats
although I were growing old by then and I said
"what" too many times but you should see me
floating on the horse turds first, then walking
deep in the thorns, then balancing on top
of the barbed wire for just to say I love you,
not to mention the heather there on the rocks
an hour north of Galway, and putting it down
on the coffee table with my other bejewels there.

Bio

What it was like to sit with Mr. Fox
on the Blvd. Raspail and negotiate
my post at Morlais, then Toulouse, then come back
in a riveted trunk with Henry Millers sewn
into my lining, Frank Sinatra to greet me
in the mile-square city, Dutch ships everywhere,
my father and mother in from Pittsburgh to give me
my French lesson, my fiancée pulling me down,
the mayor of New York God knows who, the president
asinine again, the dove I loved
in an army boot size eleven and a half and
dove or not, dove feathers or not, blood staining
the white chest, a cascade of snow come pouring
from the spruce's upper limbs, cascade, waterfall,
sheet, blanket, my mountain, your roof, your dovecote,
eating fish on the *Times*, 103rd Street,
Zoey in a corset, even then she
was a throwback—I have unlaced a corset,
and at a vanity I have sat on a stained
bench and broken my knees against art dreco
peeling wood, and there among the powders
and creams and rouges I have read Montaigne,
Locke and Hobbes, and since it was there, I read
the rituals of the Eastern Star and studied
my face in the unsilvered mirror, what about you?

Battle of the Bulge

The way a fly who dies in sugar water,
he couldn't find a way to lift his wings
out of there, they were so heavy, the way
a plant doesn't need that rich a dirt, the way
it chokes from too much love, the way
I lay on the ground, I dug a hiphole, I slept
with grass, and dirt, the way Ammon Hennacy
wore a red flannel shirt, and a tie, he was
Dorothy Day's friend—you knew the saint?—it was
my own costume for years, he was in prison
with Berkman—in Atlanta—Berkman was there
for shooting and stabbing Frick, Hennacy for
conscience; I met Hennacy on Spruce Street
in 1958, the same year I met
Jack Lindeman who lost his hearing in Belgium,
the winter of 1944, he lives in
Fleetwood, PA, and we communicate by
fax—I never heard him ask for pity
nor did we ever talk about that winter, he
introduced me to Dorothy Day and published
his poems in the *Catholic Worker*—and Marvin Hadburg,
he whom I pity, he was drafted when the
government was desperate and sent to
southern Georgia for four weeks' training
and then to Bastogne three days before Christmas
where he spent a week in a barn and came home
with both feet frozen a day or two short of two months
some of the flesh cut off, as I remember,
a gold discharge button in his lapel,
selling underwear again in his father's store,
his head very small, his shoulders hunched, his mouth
always open—I would say he was a
collector of feathers for the Achaean archer

Teucer of the incurved bow, whose shoulder
Hector smashed with a rock, just where the clavicle
leads over to the neck and breast, thus deadening
his wrist and fingers, I would say that Ajax
knocked him down when passing by and Zeus,
deflector of arrows and breaker of spears, the father
of slaughter without end, he pissed on him.

Mars

What you say bout Orson Welles his folly, his
belly full of sheepskin, liquid of ale?
What you say bout the cave on the bluff my father oh
were packing us up one night at the end of the thirties
he knew as a child-child dark-skinned Jewish bastard
he had *smoked* there tobeys you know and lukewarm
RC Cola, child-child roasted potato,
and I came home from the movie at ten o'clock
and he was packing and she for they was crazy
for caves and oh them Martians and ah them Martians,
and I saw Orson in 1950 in Paris oh,
he was directing a play and he was fat-fat
and ah he bade us welcome and how did we know?
and was it *Macbeth*? Child-child in 1950
for I love *Touch of Evil* best and worst-worst
Citizen Kane of California, Hearst-Hearst.

Driven

The only star last night was cloud-riven,
a frog said that to me, but aside from the word
"riven," which could have been "rivet" or "privet,"
for sometimes he disguises his voice, that puffed-up
goggle-eyed bug-eating monster, a machine of
sorts sitting on a pod and floating south the
way a frog floats south and he half looks
himself, and if you ask him he goes on, for
he is *driven*, I prefer it, that *driven*,
try that under your cloud, or in your big mouth,
along with steak and eggs; he says driven,
and stars are driven too, some are cloud-driven,
and some are clear and one is blue and under that
blue star I slept then I woke up
driven—I was a little dizzy, and staggered
here and there but I was driven—ah
cut his legs off and grill them, eat in the weeds
and grow two hearts, two lungs, another eye,
give yourself up for dissection, call it hiven,
better than heaven, spiders, moths, flies, frog-hiven.

Shepherd

Greece, the light of my life, but there was a man who
taught Business and one day an ex-student
from another college came to see him and she was
gorgeous enough you wanted to die, and after
thirty minutes alone they both came out
and how he sucked his pipe I could have murdered him;
but he was critical for she lay on a hillside
above new Samos and woke up to a bell for
there was a shepherd and there was a dog and after
how many minutes he fucked her with the dog
barking, and *how disgusting* my colleague said,
imagine, a filthy shepherd, and I was stunned
by the word "shepherd," it meant nothing to him;
and what the sun was like that morning, the marble
she fingered the while oh two or three thousand years
there baking and freezing, but most of all I hated
how I had to accept his version of a formal
rift in order to fight him, how I retreated
behind some broken stones, a fireplace, say,
four hundred years old, and we would have to argue
about sulfa and penicillin, I wanted to
pull the pipe out of his mouth, I wanted to
have a dog like that, a bell either tied
to his white throat or at my own neck playing
Schubert or Mahler, down on my worn-out knees.

Homesick

I was reading again and French apples
were on my mind and oranges the way they sold them
in giant carts and how the skin was thick and
loosened from the flesh and how it made an
orange saucer where you placed the sections
after you pulled the threads away, the ugly word
"pith," it's called, and raspberries with cream—
and how it would have been if I had stayed
in the same hotel another eight or ten years and
married someone else—it always comes to
that—and taken up another trade,
for as you know what we call nostalgia
is for the life we *didn't* live, so much for
homesickness, and I am homesick too for
southern Spain, where I didn't live, but mostly for
Mogador (where I didn't live) with the tiny
white streets and blue shutters, one store the
flutes on one side, the drums on the other, the synagogue
smaller than the African Methodist church
on North Governor Street in Iowa City
before they rounded us up, though we had two days,
for we had spies, to tear the linings open
and sew our jewels in and our thousand franc notes,
although we had to leave our heavy furniture
behind, and Libby's picture, when we boarded
the plane for Paris, more like the camel that took us
to live with the Berbers in the Atlas Mountains
twenty-five hundred years ago than not like,
all of whose fault it was that Ezra who preached
the ups and downs; and how the Berbers welcomed us,
and how the French put us in crowded rooms
and made us sit for hours, for they believed in
égalité, so everyone should die of

boredom equally and *Vive la France* and
Hail to the Eagle and Rah, Miss Liberty,
one of her breasts exposed—I have nostalgia
for your life too, what are you, Mongolian?
Don't leave the rugs behind, milk the horses!
Are you a Russian? You are great at this.
Light the samovar! I give you my past for
nothing. Here is your number. Line up, my lovers!

The Law

The world is always burning, you should fly
from the burning if you can, and you should hold
your head oh either above or below the dust
and you should be careful in the blocks of Bowery
below or above the Broome that always is changing
from one kind of drunkenness to another
for that is the law of suffering, and you know it.

She Was a Dove
for ANNE MARIE

Red are her eyes, for she was a dove once,
and green was her neck and blue and gray her throat,
croon was her cry and noisy flutter her wing once
going for water, or reaching up for another note.

And yellow her bill, though white some, and red her feet
though not to match her eyes for they were more suave,
those feet, and he who bore down above her
his feathers dropped around her like chaff from wheat.

And black was her mood, consider a dove that black,
as if some avian fury had overcome her
and overtaken my own oh lackadaisical state
for she was the one I loved and I abused her.

Blue we lived in, blue was our country seat,
and wrote our letters out on battered plates
and fought injustice and once or twice French-kissed there
and took each other out on desperate dates.

And it was a question always should we soar—
like eagles you know—or should we land and stay,
the battle I fought for sixty years or more
and still go over every day.

And there was a spot of orange above the bone
that bore a wing, though I could never explain
how that was what I lived and died for
or that it blossomed in the brain.

from
Save the
Last Dance

Diogenes

Diogenes for me and sleeping in a bathtub
and stealing the key to the genealogy room
close to the fake Praxiteles and ripping
a book up since the wrath had taken me
over the edge again and you understand
as no one else how when the light is lit
I have to do something, I couldn't hold my arm up
for nothing, I couldn't stand on the top step
barking—I'll put it this way, living in a room
two cellars down was good, I got to smell
the earth, I carried a long red wire down
with a bulb attached—after that it never mattered.

Traveling Backwards

Traveling backwards in time is almost nothing
for here is the brain and with it I have relived
one thing after another but I am wavering
at *only* reliving though what is hard is being there—
I don't know what the Germans called it, existing,
non-existing, both at once, there is a
rose explaining it, or it's a table;
imagine that, from one tree and its branches
once it was rooted, once the leaves were glabrous
and coruscating, then came everything.

What For?

1946 there was an overcoat
with rows of buttons fifteen dollars and two
American flags for some ungodly reason
and a slight rise in the distance as the street
went over the river for which I would have breathed
the air both in and out since I was a bellows
and one by one my lungs were ruined but I wouldn't
change my life, what for? You wouldn't know
unless you crossed the river yourself, unless you
climbed a hill and turned around twice
to stare at the street behind you, either mud
or cobblestone, and count the wooden steps
or look through the windows longingly, the houses
piled up the one below the next, the dirt
supreme, your breathing heavy, the base of a cliff
even further below, a river shining from
time to time, your mind half-empty, your teacher
a curbstone, the mountain really hill upon hill;
you know the details, the porches pulled you up,
your face turned white at a certain point, I'm sure
you walked through a cloud how slow you learned, how absurd
the goats of Arcady or the baskets of apples
in New Jerusalem compared to that.

Bronze Roosters

How love of every single human creature
took place in my life and how it lasted for almost
a week but I had a fever; and the day
I realized finally I had to give up
running for I had lost the will, almost the
muscles themselves, I was confused since I
was never a runner as an adult, and on the
last day I was taking my antibiotics
I lost a small pink pill while in between
reading the labels, or I convinced myself
that that was the case and it took me almost an hour
to stop my coughing I was in such a state,
and I was light-headed walking over the bricks
and had to hold onto my wooden fence, amazed
that we could last the way we do compared to
birds just blown by the wind, their locomotion
beyond themselves, or ants and beetles, God,
what does the mind do there, or bronze roosters?

Blue Like That

She was a darling with her roses, though what I
like is lavender for I can dry it and
nothing is blue like that, so here I am,
in my arms a bouquet of tragic lavender,
the whole history of southern France against my
chest, the fields stretching out, the armies
killing each other, horses falling, Frenchmen
dying by the thousands, though none for love.

59 N. Sitgreaves

As if some creature down there was having a smoke
and there was a lamp with fringes and a rug
so filthy the earth was red and the blue flowers
were black and there was nothing to read and only
a shovel in my face, for such it is
under the lid that I rocked forever and changed
my clay pipe every hour; and reading what
was left of the Psalms, for they were torn and eaten,
I did so by holding a candle over my head;
and I was careful of water for in Them it says
God is filled with water and in Them it says
the valleys shout with joy, which I do here;
and also I whistle in spite of the dirt in my mouth,
and I still hate oppression and I hate slander
where there was a brick outhouse and a library
down from the kitchen and the butchered backyard maple.

Spaghetti

Not infrequently destroyed as bits of paper
of no value by the women in my family,
namely Ida, Libby, and the maid Thelma,
my drawings were gone by the time I was eleven
and so I turned to music and led orchestras
walking through the woods; and Saturday nights
we feasted on macaroni, tomato soup and falso
cheese cooked at three hundred fifty degrees
which I called spaghetti until I was twenty-one
and loved our nights there, Thelma, Libby, and Ida,
fat as I was then, fat and nearsighted
and given over to art, such as I saw it,
though smothered somewhat by the three of them;
and it would be five years of breaking loose,
reading Kropotkin first, then reading Keats,
and standing on my head and singing by which
I developed the longing, though I never
turned against that spaghetti, I was always
loyal to one thing, you could almost measure
my stubbornness and my wildness by that loyalty.

Love

A part of me eats her fingers and a part of me
soaks the dishes but I hate to be scattered
for that is why it took so long and with my
hands enbubbled like that it's up to her
mostly and I resist for I have the counter
still to scrub and I have a wet
dish towel in my hand as we walk up
eleven steps to the landing followed by six
for in the latter part of my life I'm counting
and nothing, nothing, is sweeter than her protest
or mine, for we are protestants and lie there
hours on end protesting, that is love,
in her house and mine, both the same except that
I have two sets of stairs, a front and a back,
so counting is endless, at least it's multiple,
and you know multiple and what it goes with.

Before Eating

Here's to your life
and here's to your death

and here's to coughing
and here's to breath.

Here's to snowfall
here's to flurry,

here's your hat,
what's your hurry?

Here's to judge,
here's to Jewry,

here's to beer,
here's to brewery.

Leave me alone,
I want to worry;

make me lamb chops,
make me curry.

Here's to Voigt,
here's to Bidart,

here's getting off
to a running start.

Here's to Dove,
here's to Levine,

here's to the graveyards
in Berlin and Wien.

Here's to Gilbert
who learned it from me,

here's to the ninety-foot
Christmas tree

he fell on his head from
shortening his height,

here's to the grimness
of his grim night;

and I could go on for
forty pages,

listing my joys
and listing my rages,

but I should stop
while I'm still ahead

and make my way
to my own crooked bed;

so here's to the end,
the final things,

and here's to forever
and what that brings,

and here's to a cup of
coffee in the winter

and here's to the needle,
and here's to the splinter.

And here's to the pear tree
I couldn't live without,

and here's to its death
I wrote about

from 1966
to 1972,

a kind of root
from which I grew,

and here's to the fruit—
I like that too,

bruised and juicy
through and through,

and here's to the core
oh most of all

and how I chewed it
from Mall to Mall

and how I raddled
the stem in my teeth

as if it were wind
against a red leaf;

and here's to the wind
and here's to your eyes

and here's to their honey,
dark as the skies

and here's to the silk roof
over your head

and here's to the pillows
and here's to the bed

and here's to your plaid robe,
and here's to your breast,

and here's to your new coat
and here's to your vest

and your fine mind and its desire,
as wild and crazy as the fire

we saw burning going home in the dark,
driving by and wanting to park,

but stopped by sirens and flashing lights—
wild nights, wild nights,

a pine tree in the other lane,
cones exploding in my brain.

Asphodel

He was dead so he was only a puff
of smoke at the most and I had to labor to see him
or just to hear and when we spoke it was as
if we were waiting in the rain together
or in a shelter on 96th Street or by the
side of a train in Washington, D.C., say,
changing engines and patting each other's stomachs
by way of intimacy, and he said what he
wanted most of all, when it came to trains,
was merely to stand on the platform looking out
the dirty window at the water beyond
the row of houses or the stand of trees
for it was *distance* he loved now and the smell of
the ocean, even more than coffee, but it was
only *concoction* for he didn't have the senses
anymore, and I forgot to say that
he was a veteran and he wore a green cap
that had KOREA VETERAN printed on the face
with three bright battle ribbons below the lettering,
and I forgot to say his ears were large,
the way it sometimes happens in older men,
though he was dead, and he was on the train with
his wife who had red hair of sorts and a dress
that spread out like a tassel of silk, and war
was what we talked about and what the flowers
were the way a poppy was the emblem
of World War I and we both laughed at how
there were no flowers for Korea nor any
poems for that matter though he was sad and although
he wore the hat he said it was a stupid
useless war, unlike Achilles Odysseus
talked to in Hell, who loved his war and treasured
the noses he severed and the livers he ruptured,

and picture them selling their asphodel in front of
a supermarket or a neighborhood bank
and picture us waiting until our ears were long
just to hate just one of their dumb butcheries.

What Then?

You know I know there is just enough light
between the boards and that the tree creaked and
the branches scraped against the roof, and all I
can think about is whether my shoes will be covered
with dust when all is said and done or whether
the cake will cover it and cracked and brittle
they rise once again as all shoes rise
both high and dry if even the tongue is split,
and what was called a leather top was loose
from its moorings; you know the pain the shoe
itself swelling can cause here, how can we rid
the world of swelling, that was my first grievance,
or muck to start with, muck was the problem, no one
I know should die but what do my two black shoes
know, let's say a creature will blow them dry
by beating his wings or let's say we'll walk next time
say north instead of south, oh nearer my face
to thee and nearer your face to me, what then?

One Poet

As if one poet then who was in his sixties
I wanted to tell him that I read his book
and how I lingered on one page and couldn't
go to the next, I had to read it again,
and later I kissed it, but I couldn't tell him that
nor did I ever write, since I lost his
letter, I remember putting it in
my inside pocket with the colored pens
and how it must have slipped out as I ran
down the four steps and over the forsythia
looking for my keys; and at the annual
ceremonies somewhere close I think to
Gramercy Park he barked at me not knowing
how much I loved his work nor did he see
out of the dusty window left of the cloakroom
how a dog had severed the head of a pigeon
and how its bloody feathers lay on the sidewalk
and blood was on the dog's round face and how
oddly he growled and how he licked his lips.

Wordsworth

More than anything else it was
the smell of dead birds that overpowered
you as you walked into that woods
and everything else was sheer bullshit
including the violets you picked in the openings
and tied in small bouquets holding
your nose withal as if you truly
had someone to give a posy to, and there
was either a wolf or there wasn't, it doesn't matter
now, for it was second or third growth,
and it was more scrag than not and anyhow
it's house to house now ugly fucking streets
where once da da da da and you were beautiful
innocent young though you were fat and clumsy
too but you were you and you treasured the blue nosegay.

Lorca

The fact that no one had ever seen Lorca run
had only to do with the legend of his clumsiness
for one foot was shorter than the other and he was
terrified to cross the street by himself,
though dogs barking in the mountains above him
brought him back to his senses and caused him
when he was alone to try leaping and skipping
the way you did; and he tried the hop, skip, and jump
he learned from the 1932 Olympics
and loaded the left side of his mouth with green tobacco
when he was only eleven for he took comfort
in every form of degradation; and it was
in John Jay Hall in 1949
that Geraldo from Pittsburgh made a personal connection
for they were both housed in room 1231
twenty years apart not counting the months,
and only one of them heard Eisenhower give his maiden speech
outside the courtyard entrance, and there were bitter
oranges enough for them both, and you can imagine
one of our poets in the hands of our own bastards,
but what is the use of comparing, only the hats
are different—though I'm not too sure—the roses
maybe they stuffed in our mouths—the Granadas.

Death by Wind

As for those who face their death by wind
and call it by the weird name of forgiveness
they alone have the right to marry birds,
and those who stopped themselves from falling down
by holding the wall up or the sink in place
they can go without much shame for they
have lived enough and they can go click, click
if they want to, they can go tok, tok
and they can marry anything, even hummingbirds.

Rose in Your Teeth

Rose in your teeth, my darling, rose in your teeth,
and blood on your hands and shoes on your feet,
and barefoot in mud and how the shoes went floating
on bodies of water, I sold them at Baker's and Burt's
and carried the boxes on high; and there were women
galore who sat there in rows in their chairs on their thrones
in stockings of silk, and we rolled by on wagons of wood
and counted till midnight in codes and by numbers and letters,
and I did the forms though once I led the charge
and I was the priest for two or three hours; and there were
forgotten styles in colors you couldn't imagine
and heels of the past and folded tongues and such,
and I was hungry at one in the morning and ate
forgotten foods, and can't you tell how I
was a woman then and ransacked the upper shelves
and how I ran for the money and remembered
twelve to fourteen numbers and I knew
the stock and detested the manager and kept
my own tallies and ate my sandwich from a bag
during the later days of the war and just after,
when there were murder gardens everywhere.

Save the Last Dance for Me

When it comes to girls the Chihuahua
on Ninth Street going down to
Washington on the left side
below the Hong Kong Fruit,
he knows where he's going, between their
beautiful legs, his eyes
bulge a little, his heart,
because he is small, surges,
explodes too much, he is
erotic, his red tongue
is larger than a squirrel's, but
not too much, nor does he
walk on a wire with fresh
ricotta in his mouth nor
an apple they sell for a quarter,
a bit of rot on one side but
sweet underneath the skin, more
McIntosh than not, he
loves Velveeta, he knows
the price of bananas, he whines
when there is a death; there was one
drowning in a sewer,
his owner gave me five dollars
for lifting the lid with a hammer
and going down into the muck
when I was twelve, it was
my first act of mercy
and she gave me a towel
that matched the Chihuahua's towel
and ah he trembled containing
such knowledge and such affection
and licked my face and forced me
to shut my eyes, it was
so much love, his whole

body was shaking and I,
I learned from him and I
learned something once from a bird
but I don't know his name
though everyone I tell it to
asks me what his name was
and it is shameful, what
was he, a dog? The Klan
was flourishing all the while
we dreamed of hydroelectric
so we were caught in between
one pole and another and
we were Hegelian or just
Manichaean, we kept
the hammer on top of the manhole
so we could lift it to get
our softballs and tennis balls
though he who weighed a pound
could easily fall into
the opening, such was our life
and such were our lives the last
few years before the war when
there were four flavors of ice cream
and four flavors only; I'll call him
Fatty; I'll call him Peter;
Jesús, I'll call him, but only
in Spanish, with the "h" sound,
as it is in Mexico;
Jesús, kiss me again,
Jesús, you saved *me*,
Jesús, I can't forget you;
and what was her name who gave me
the towel? and who was I?
and what is love doing in
a sewer, and how is disgrace
blurred now, or buried?

from
In Beauty Bright

February 22

Reading a Japanese novel during the one day of
sunshine following a week of rain, my daughter-in-law
going to the post office for the new stamps
and on her way home though it was winter and
bitter weather was on the way she found a
buttercup which meant, she said, the Arctic
ice cap was melting and it was getting warmer
except we couldn't resist it and we walked
back through the streaks of ice and the mud for buttercups
are varnished, and we adore them, though we mostly
live in fear and, for that matter, we crawled
back and on the way I smashed the knuckles
of my left hand on the blue stone wall
for Ronald Reagan and Donald Duck had made it
but neither had Scott Nearing or Emma Goldman,
talk about nincompoops, talk about birthdays.

Stoop

While on a stoop and eating boiled beef
and while my hands are dripping with horseradish
and while a crescent moon reflects itself
in one of the windows on Sixth Avenue
near what used to be the great Balducci's
across from the women's prison and the library,
though truth the sky is blue so it is probably
April and it's probably twenty, thirty
years ago, and I was studying women's
shoes before the long point killed the two
end toes the same time I was killing time
before the meeting at the Waverly
inside a window as I recall for I had a
burden then and I was given to meetings
like that though even then I knew what it was
like to be free of burdens for I was part
mule, wasn't I, therefore I knew what freedom
was and I am mule to this day and carry a
weight, and I will to the grave—you will see me
put it into the hole first, it is so cumbersome,
with ears the color of the sun and compromised
by wings, which I am too, and there's one mule
I knew in the late thirties whose name was Molly,
alas, not Sal, and she wasn't stupid and she was
hardly stubborn and she loved apple trees
and she was wise and loving, above rubies.

Aliens

How on the river the loosestrife has taken over,
and how at the wedding there were spaghetti straps
and one or two swollen bellies, and the judge who
married them was wearing red sneakers and he was
altogether a little pompous, and how the
Guatemalans have moved into the borough
and they are picked up in front of the Flower Mart
sitting by the ice machine and there the
bargaining takes place and both sides love
light maybe because of the glittering
between the trees and locked inside the droplets,
and what the swollen river is up to and how
New York City is stealing the water and what,
with the weather events, there could be a failure
of one or more of New York's three earthen dams
or there could be a collapse of the steel tunnel
feeding the city, and what the language is
they argue with and whether it's under the table
the way they get paid or there are watermarked checks
with complicated deductions, and what the birds are
that eat the garbage and if a plastic milk box
turned upside down is not a good enough table
for coffee and doughnuts especially if the sugar
goes neatly through the holes and red plastic
makes music too and boots take the place of sneakers.

Dumb

Fleabane again and I have another year
to take up its redness and what the wayside is like
with or without it and I have another year
to charge across the wooden bridge and shake it
again and take on the animals and fight
the stupid bikes and the bikers who ride across
with their legs spread out instead of walking their bikes
so we didn't have to be pushed against the rails,
they are so dumb and their bikes have so many dumb
and useless gears like a dumb idiot box
with two thousand stations, only dumb ancient
boxing and ancient movies worth anything,
Jack Johnson or Marciano, even
Orson Welles too much, give me the unself-
conscious, Karl Malden or Jean Harlow,
for this is an old flower, it hates whatever
it wants to, it grows where it wants and it
loves goats because of their flattened eyes.

Gracehoper

In the way Ovid lectured a green grasshopper
and all the grasshopper did was spit up tobacco,
in the way he begged for food for he was the first
bohemian, though he detested the brutal word
gracehoper, see James Joyce, and when two ants
ran around the corner when it was dinner
and how the gracehoper wept and it was cold
on top of the cold stone wall though dinner cost
at most say twenty cents, and how the ants
reasoned, and how the gracehoper, and what the stakes
were, and what the dream was, see Aesop.

Sugar

How when I cut the giant Norway maple down
the first warm day the stump was covered in sap
and I ended up stuffing Russian sage
into my Polish nose and waving medicine
down and around the stump which in this case
was more like grass than it was a bush I picked
the other side of the bridge so I could consider
the other side of beauty for a while,
though when I saw the maggots all I could think of
was dead flesh and maggot therapy
and how the maggots stink and struggling bees
swimming in the syrup came up for air from
time to time but it was murder there
and there was murder everywhere and stumps
galore and broken this and that and smashed
everything I was supposed to venerate.

Sinai

No one thought of naming his dog Sinai
for fear of offending the mountain, given how dogs
whimpered and growled outside the tents, their ribs
glistening in the fire, their tongues dripping
oh centuries before we clothed them and let them sleep
on our mattresses and named them Miriam and even
in one case I know Moses, more for his croupy
bark than anything else, for he was the one
that had the problem—though there were other mountains
and one was named Chicora after the poem
I wrote in 1944 though there was
never a dog by that name and that was a mountain
you ran up, it was so perfect, and at the top
above the chained-down cabin the stunted trees
bowed and groveled for they were dogs, and Sinai,
since she was not Misty and not Lucille, just whistled.

Domestic

It was as if his gills were going in and out
and there was a croaking noise he made that scared her
almost to death he imitated while lying
under her heavy salty blanket she pulled
up to his neck and tucked in at his sides
for she was going to read a little afterwards
and put her glasses on that perched on the edge
of her English nose and held her head in her hand
while he took in, for a second only, the streaks
of lightning mixed with the moonlight as if one brightness
was not enough, two gods he thought, and how the
river would smell tomorrow as he swam over
the greasy rocks and she would take him again
in her brackish arms that more than reading and more than
music it was she overcame her sorrow,
and that is why her elbows were sore and the rotten
underwater steps gave way and love
rushed into her mouth and mercy broke over her head.

Frogs

The part that we avoided was not the heart
but what we called the pouch, for it still swelled
or seemed to and there was plenty of horror cutting
into what made the music or at least
the agency you might call it, and more than one of us
retched and as you know, that can become
contagious—think of a roomful of pouches exploding
think of the music on a summer night
with no one conducting and think of how warm it might be
and how love songs may have gotten started there.

In Beauty Bright

In beauty bright and such it was like Blake's
lily and though an angel he looked absurd
dragging a lily out of a beauty bright store
wrapped in tissue with a petal drooping,
nor was it useless—you who know it know
how useful it is—and how he would be dead
in a minute if he were to lose it though
how do you lose a lily? *His* lily was white
and he had a foolish smile there holding it up like
a candelabrum in his right hand facing the
mirror in the hall nor had the endless
centuries started yet nor was there one thorn
between his small house and the beauty bright store.

Journey

How dumb he was to wipe the blood from his eye
where he was sucker punched and stagger out
onto the plaza blind. He had been waiting
all night for the acorn moon and eating pineapple
topping over his ice cream and arguing
either physics or philosophy. He thinks,
at this late date, it was the cave again
throwing a shadow, although it may have been
only some way of reconciling the two
oblivious worlds, which was his mission anyhow—
if only there was a second moon. He had a
kind of beard and though he could practically lift
the front end of a car and was already
reading Blake, he had never yet tasted honey.

Died in the Mills

Then, fifty dollars for a Hungarian
say a black dress to go to the funeral
and shoes with soles for the three oldest, that leaves
a dollar fifty for the feast but I'd say
what a dollar was worth then you could have
a necktie if you wanted and paprikash
for twenty or thirty and strudel with apples and nuts
and violins—he favored the violin—
and it is not just poets who love meadows
and take their sneakers off and their socks to walk
on the warm rocks and dip their tender white feet
in the burning freezing water and then bend down
precariously to pick up a froglet and sight
the farthest lonely tree and note the wind
moving quickly through the grasses their last summer.

Rosenblatt

The most revolting thing of all was carrying
a suitcase through the gate for that was mixing
your journeys, even wearing an overcoat
or socks—with clocks—inside your shoes was stupid,
but nothing compared to a suitcase, amazing compartments
for matching neckties and handkerchiefs, and one
for underwear and one for toilet articles
which when it was forced open—for who had such
a tiny key—there was your name burned in
the leather, nor did the scalloped bottles spill,
dear Rosepetal, son of the Hamburg kosher fishmonger.

Iberia

I have been here so long I remember Salazar
and how he tortured my four main poets in Portugal
with his "moral truth and patriotic principles,"
and fatherless Coughlin and all the old bastards
that stretched in one great daisy chain from the coast
of California east and east to New York and
London and thence across Eurasia to God knows
what small moral and patriotic islands
so listen to me for once and hate for good
all moral islands, and if you haven't done so
already add my Pessoa to your Lorca.

Independence Day

There were packs of dogs to deal with and broomsticks
whacking rubber balls and everyone stopping for
aeroplanes and chasing fire engines
and standing around where sidewalks on hills turned almost
level, and horses and horseshit, and ice in the cellars;
and Saturday I wore a dark suit and leaned
against my pillar and Sunday I put on a necktie
and stood in front of a drugstore eating a Clark bar.
The 4th of July I stayed in my attic resting in
filthy cardboard and played with my bats, I stretched
their bony wings, and put a burning match
to the bundle of papers, especially to the ropes
that held them together and read the yellow news
as it went up in smoke and spoke for the fly and raged
against the spider, say what you will, and started
my drive to Camden to look at the house on Mickle Street
and walked—with him—down to the river to skip
some stones, since Ty Cobb did it and Jim Thorpe did it
though it was nothing compared to George Washington
throwing silver dollars, and for our fireworks
we found some brown beer bottles and ran down Third Street
screaming, but he had to go back home and sit
in his rocking chair for there was a crowd of Lithuanians
coming and he was a big hit in Vilnius
the way he sat in his mound of papers and gripped
the arms, though I was tired of Lithuanians
who didn't know shit, not to mention Romanians,
to pick a country out of a hat—or I was
just tired and Anne Marie was right, I shouldn't
be driving at night, I should be dead, I don't
even know how to give instructions, I don't even know
my rabbi's name—she and her motorcycle—

imagine them speaking Babylonian over
my shoe box—imagine them throwing flowers—fleabane,
black-eyed Susans, daisies—along with the dirt.

The Name

Having outlived Allen I am the one who
has to suffer New York all by myself and
eat my soup alone in Poland although
sometimes I sit with Linda he met in Berkeley
or San Francisco when he met Jack, the bread
just coarse enough, the noodles soft but not
thin and wasted, and not too salty the way the
Chinese farther down sometimes make them, the
name still on my mind whatever the reason for
mystery, or avoidance, though rat Netanyahu
and pig that swings from a needle or lives in some
huge incubator, they do darkness where there
was light, the *name* hates them, the *name*
in hiding, the *name* with a beard, and Linda she
loves the *name* though she invokes her Christ
as Jack her lover and tormentor did and
taught her to do though it is too easy, that,
it troubles me but what can I say, what *should* I
say while we walk north on the right-hand side,
past the pork store and the hardware store, me lecturing
on Logos (my God) and whatnot Hebrews and Greeks
where Allen and I once kissed, Jack in the sun now.

Broken Glass

Broken bottles brought him to Mickle Street
and pieces of glass embedded in the mud
to Whitman's wooden house across the street from
the Church of the Most Unhappy Redeemer for when
it was too quiet he broke another bottle
and he collected his glass in a paper bag
and when he was *verloren* he cut himself
though just as like he cut himself on a wall
while doing an exercise to stretch the tendons
so he could get rid of the numb and burning feeling,
or sometimes he sat on a hydrant and once on a bench
with drooping slats so when the slats gave his back
also gave and feeling came back to his foot
as it came back to Whitman when he sat
on the orange rush seats or rocked in his chair between
the visits and loved the hollyhocks that grew
in the cracks and for a nickel the whole republic
would turn to broken glass as Oscar insisted.

Soll Ihr Gornisht Helfen
Nothing Will Help

Some Austrian Jew or other who dipped his head
in Christian Water so he could get a job
in Wien or some such place, whose cousins galore
never dipped, never stripped,
for they were Jewish through and through
and carried their suitcases into the blue
whatever the gossamer gowns *they* wore
though it didn't help a bit,
all that shit
for he had a leather suitcase too,
Austrian Jew.

Voltage

I don't know one thing from another but I
think the one on the left is a television wire
and the one on which the blue jay jumps is electric
though how they plan the flow to go up the bricks
or right across the yard it's one of the secrets
and I am learning something about high voltage
and insulation and the different kinds of
poles and I do like the small and crooked ones;
and when the wires were put in conduits I even
grieved for I like torture to be in the open
and cruelty, or indifference, not to be buried
like oral agreements in some small living room,
and I am beginning even to like Verizon and
Sprint, loose and hanging multiple wires
every which way, for in a decade from now
I could grow nostalgic for the metal
footrests and the signs we nailed on poles
for parties and sales or the uphill walk
in Nebraska underneath the endless rows
and what remained of the messages, a cry
from Red Eugene or Red Emma, Mumford
swallowing his sword, never a word
from Stockholm, though a little later the rodents
made their speeches and got their millions, and those
were masters of the underground pipes and conduits
and loved their secrecy and spoke with accents
here and there and were invited to castles
and added fees to their prizes lovingly
and watched their backs of course because you never
know when the hot blue murderous currents will get you.

For D.

Let not a grocery bag of bloody napkins come between us.
Or a floor covered with cigarette butts and dirty underwear
or an alcoholic son or a paper with your
instructions regarding the upper and lower keyholes.

. . .

Let me not be a part of yet another creative narrative.

. . .

Come now the love.

. . .

Come now the two-inch predator wasp dragging a huge insect
over the rocky sidewalk into his dark hole under the porch.

. . .

Come the bees now clinging to flowered curtains.

Rage

I lost my rage while helping a beetle recover
and stood there with precision, balancing
grass with stone and lifted my stick to show
how dirt holds us up and what is indifferent and what
their music could be and what the whistling train,
according to childhood and ecstatic age.

Love

I loved your sweet neck but I loved your shoulder blades more
and wondered whether I should kiss your cheek first
or your hair for I was watching carefully, and
sitting on the edge of the tub I thought of
the three great places, namely the three gardens
of Eve, Gypsy Rose Lee, and Mrs. Bloom
lately of Auschwitz, though there are others, oh
there are others, but show me the two hands concealing
love and you have the whole history of the human race there.

Nostalgia

Stalin comes to mind who tried to destroy
everything they remembered, including the tree
they ate from, green delicious, including the store
they stole from after school, including the water
they leaned their foreheads on the moss for and even
the blue stone that once diverted the river
and by so doing came loose and was for the two
long months a dangerous step, but not the bulldozer.

Sleeping with Birds

I have slept with a Crow and a Robin and it's
not easy, birds, nor going to the airport without
a passport nor singing for security
something out of Noël Coward and thus
proving you're English and telling them you're on the way
to catch a bird; but you had to take your shoes off
anyhow and they put a stick up your groin
and one down your throat and you made walrus noises
to show your suffering.
                And it was Crete
you traveled in and she had a withered wing
from being crushed by a horse when she was thirteen;
and what you remember is how she sobbed after
climbing into the bus and putting her suitcase
into the overhead bin, but I am conflating
trips and even conflating birds though this one
was named Mavis and she wrote long letters
for she was English, and her last name was Sparrow.

My Libby

I hung onto her likeness and centered it
but as far as the samovar
they threw it into the river
when they took a raft somewhere
or just they bought someone *else's* keepsakes,
and as far as the chest
of hand-sewn sheets and pillowcases
they set it on fire
and floated it into West Virginia
but I who came for the light
I learned to sing and put my back out of place
by reading on the floor
for I was either the first or second generation
depending on how you counted
and I could have once become a Quaker
and now I have to confess
that it was I who hung them up to dry
and folded them in the dark
for here you have to fight for life.

86th Birthday at MacDowell

Why do you always climb an extra pair of stairs
to get to a good light and why does all your pain—
speaking only of backaches—always show in your neck,
and do you think it only shows there or also under the pouch
of your left eye, and can't you just cut your neck off?

And what is the age of your fellow artists shrieking from
their crowded table and shouldn't I be working all day
with Alessandra changing words from thirty years ago
to make myself more musical and when will she be
done with Einstein's bastardly life and ready to give herself
to my fine animal, vegetable and human love songs?

Plaster Pig

It didn't work that the bores I grew up with
smeared my door with lard
for I was enlightened and walked with the rest
in the mountains of Italy on Easter morning
and went to St. John's on Christmas Eve;
and neither does anyone I know
keep a plaster pig in his living room
for it is not what goes into the snout,
and you will forgive me
whether you like it or not
for wasn't it being *afraid* of the pig
that drove us there in the first place
and wasn't it God in the second,
and it had bristles in the third,
and the lungs were too small
and it was as smart as a fox terrier
and lived in shit.
And it turns wild in a second like nothing else
and someone once told me the male
has a cock that twists around like a corkscrew
and for those reasons I won't eat it.

Apt. 5 FW I

We return to the blood pudding
every chance we get
that every poet in Kraków
knows just as he knows the cabbage,
so fok the five flights
and the door to the roof
and the plaster ceiling since
my left arm hung down and scribbled
on the gray and green and yellow painted floor;
and there was a wind in the airshaft
and a red and blue beacon I said of Empire
that Schechter called the Divine Light
so give me back my Chinese landlady and my orange bathtub.

Counting

You remind me always it's thirteen years
though when I sit with my calendar or after
with just my fingers I can't remember or just
confuse myself by trying to put my things
in order but I am almost always wrong
and I have to empty the room and pull the blinds down
and fold up the rug and sweep the floor
and put a wooden chair under the window
so I can think by squeezing the rungs until
the veins in my hands turn blue, for in the beginning
I climbed into your car and two weeks later
though neither of us gave it a thought we walked
across the street for breakfast where there was an ocean
nearby and that's the morning we started counting.

Day of Grief

I was forcing a wasp to the top of a window
where there was some sky and there were tiger lilies
outside just to love him or maybe only
simply a kiss for he was hurrying home
to fight a broom and I was trying to open
a door with one hand while the other was swinging
tomatoes, and you could even smell the corn
for corn travels by wind and there was the first
hint of cold and dark though it was nothing
compared to what would come, and someone should mark
the day, I think it was August 20th, and
that should be the day of grief for grief
begins then and the corn man starts to shiver
and crows too and dogs who hate the wind
though grief would come later and it was a relief
to know I wasn't alone, but be as it may,
since it was cold and dark I found myself singing
the brilliant love songs of my other religion.

Droit de Faim

Once I was a postwar doctoral student
eating a sandwich on the sly in one of the
nethermost aisles of an empty superette
on Broadway near 100th in the days of
unchecked books and I could cut my bread
and put on mayonnaise in a tenth of a second
and eat while walking in the direction of
the glass door, and though it's hard to explain
except in terms of hunger, or you might say
"*droit de faim*," though I would have said I was
St. John and I was in an El Greco painting
creating a world and I would have stuck to my story
even if I was slapped on the back of the neck
on the way to number this or that for I was
stubborn as the rind that covered the meat
or as the hardened skin of calf tongue stuck
in my throat I reached my fingers down to
carefully pull away from the windpipe it must have
wrapped itself around so I could breathe
again after almost a minute and thus continue
forty-six more years, or let's say forty-
five and counting, in a world I adored
on a crowded hillside on the Delaware
inside a converted 1840s schoolhouse,
and there were other brutal happenings.

1946

One hand was holding the rail and one hand
was pushed up to the middle of his back
as if it were growing there, and he was disastrous
from looking too much backwards and from loving
slums too much, including the beans he ate
and the ketchup he spiced them with; and there were musicians
busting violins and bashing trombones
who also loved the slums and they had hands
too growing on their backs nor was there a suit
to fit them or a sweater and even their heads
were turned backwards, mostly because of the rivers
they once swam in and mostly because they tossed
their girlfriends over their heads or under their legs
in someone's small enlightened living room
or at Tom's Bar where beer was still a nickel,
before they raised everything to a dime,
including doughnuts and coffee and subway fares,
ruining our lives—the bastards—it almost killed us.

Bio III

I will go down in history without a hotel
for I have been dispersed, though what I wanted
was nothing, a box for my mail, a key,
an easy chair and a floor lamp with tufted string,
a coffee shop with access inside and outside
next to the lobby with a redheaded waitress.

I was waylaid, given what I was, by
two thousand books and a Plymouth station wagon
thirty feet long and easily twelve years old
that I could carry a piano in and park
anywhere I wanted, given the year then.

And I had a bench where I could think it through
when there were two seconds of silence in between
the delivery trucks, before my coffee got cold
and the crumbs on my lip were gobbled up by sparrows
catty-corner from St. Andrew's Episcopal
where there is opera music four times a year
and you put clothes on the porch to give to the poor
—if I could compare one life to another—
though what I loved always got in the way.

from
Divine
Nothingness

Bio IV

I created an unassailable Utopia amidst Max Factor the powder
and sang such that I entertained a small living room
full mostly of berouged women in the days of Bobby Breen,
and played for money nine-ball instead of reading Kant
offering my substance to suffer by inattention and suffer
again by the final wiping out of the cosmic mirror.

And I fought Figgy Dutch the toughest when I was only ten
and then again when I was twenty but never once
though I had a gift did I pluck his red eye out,
which brought me to my kitchen window in the autumn of many a year
and many a cat hiding behind the orange and purple chrysanthemums
and one time blue not far from the birdbath his blue Santiago.

I stood there thinking not of Kant but of Paul Goodman though more
    of Delmore Schwartz and even more of John Berryman have you
    heard the terrible news?
Though ten years earlier I sat on a heated glass floor in stack after stack
for the government loved me and gave me more time than you can
    imagine,
which I used wisely not ever sleeping not ever joining the
Communist Party eating supper for a maximum of sixty cents a plate.

Crossroads I had but it meant nothing and though I went
left and right I only followed a thumbtack, and it's
amazing how I didn't die, three times, and where I woke up
and what the dogs said and how I thought Immanuel Kant
would clear the air for me for I heard it somewhere
and followed that thumbtack wherever I thought it would
take me by holding his book under my armpit
through the tunnels and up the evil hills,
beloved hills, and read in bars and restaurants,
and once in the North Side *bibliothèque* oh Scotchman oh beard

of ages nor was I ever deprived—I couldn't be deprived—
and if I dropped my Air Corps khakis down the incinerator

I never dropped my thumbtack into whose steel or tin
but shining I primped or at least I stared while waiting
for a light or waiting for a drink or looking through
my set of keys (I have eight) in the act of opening
one of my doors (I have three) which is
one of my numbers as eight is the other since I am

occult, though you'd never know it, and willing
to imitate the believer the lover, which isn't
mockery but putting on the dead clothes and giving them life by
climbing or just by breathing as we breathe into a paper bag
or into what we call rubber since our lungs are pumps
and we do the motion of arms and legs as with a threadbare

tire the left hand fitting it into place the right hand
holding the bumper jack a shoulder even
keeping the car upright the smell of birds
escaping from the woods my good luck to find
two bricks to keep the car from rolling, birdfoot
violets for luxury a gust of wind for love.

Ruth

There was a way I could find out if Ruth
were still alive but it said nothing about
her '46 Mercury nor how the gearshift ruined
our making love nor how her brother found her
compromised and what the contempt was
he registered, though I wanted to remember
the two hundred steps I climbed and the first
kisses in the empty kitchen a lifetime
before she died of emphysema and all
her credits were spread out on a page
in what they called an "almanac" for which
I chose to walk uphill for a half hour
until I reached a house with a blue boat
in the front yard, then walk back down for downhill
you are relieved since you have a whole city
below you and you have the wind at your back
for consolation and a small porcupine
at home in the empty street and hunched over
eating a rotten cabbage since grief is your subject.

Dolly

It's true that in spite of the sign that said
No Dogs or Else
I was offered a room under the weather vane
where the arrow's shadow came and went and
there was a mattress against the wall
and boxes of records and cartons of lightbulbs
and Dolly whom I hid in a shopping bag
only allowed herself to whimper
for dogs know when it's time to hide
and, for all I know, can read our miserable signs
and what you do with a dog in a shopping bag
you can gently hold her mouth shut
for she wants to bark
and that would ruin your nap on the filthy mattress
and later your swim
and most of all near the ivy and the beach plum
the race to restore knowledge with a stick.

D.

My Deborah was a judge too
only I am pulling names out of a hat
the way you did rabbits

and though she stood with her toes pointed in
as if she were in the docks
she was still the judge and would remain one.

There is only one other person who understands this,
the rest will have to go by language alone.

Think of a meadowlark you held in the cup of your hands
and how you reached down to kiss her wet feathers
and she bit you twice, on the lip and the left cheek.

Limping

Space again for a predatory wasp
to sing you to sleep and good cracks in the sidewalk
where the trees spread year by year creating broken
steps either up or down and two garages
from 1929, I know it as sure as
I know the hollow blocks though I'd have to
get into urban archaeology from
Pittsburgh east as well as the decades and that's
not my job, though I don't know what my job is,
mourning, finding a word, finding
a number—8—showing what's despicable,
clearing the air, remembering, though not official,
I'm not official, I just ingest,
devour, I said once "reconciling
two oblivious worlds," I said "getting ready,"
naming names, maybe it's
hiding behind a tree, maybe
getting inside the tree, maybe
learning to love the one or two breeds of dogs
I didn't love before—say boxers, say stiff-haired
small brown crossbreeds, say it's
walking again as far as the Flea, say it's
limping, even if I don't have to.

Love

A wet towel so many times you'd think
I'd finally get it, say the day
I reached into my pocket for two hundred fifty
with nothing in writing and forty more for the paint
though it was more for Jack Daniel's and Jim Beam;

or say the day I made the mortgage payment
to save a house and made an agreement for working
against the money, involving receipts and deadlines,
but both were ignored, and who paid the next month's mortgage
there's no way of knowing;

                                    but money is only water,
isn't it, and everything rises and falls and
somehow it's only smoke but the poorer poor
reach down on the sidewalk for a penny, bohemians
too, they know exactly what's in their pockets
down to the dollar, for they are provident,
unlike the bastards who don't need pockets since
the tailors cut their pants without to give a
smooth ferocious look like the czarist police,
or the corporate piggery eating and vomiting;

and one time I picked up a soul near Easton, PA,
and drove him down to my house and cooked
an omelette you can't imagine—with Big Boy tomatoes
out of our garden and new potatoes and drove him
downstream to catch a bus to Philadelphia
and probably gave him twenty bucks besides—
the day of hopeless amour on the Delaware.

Top of a Mountain

You could mistake the wind itself for a voice
though no one ever said it was a tenor
or not or even male or female although
without even blinking you knew, and it was mostly
unequivocal though I wanted the words,
even if it was the wind, for which, well,
a pine tree took me in her arms the way they
do and we did Fred Allen and Arthur Godfrey
and other voices back of the bus and such,
the pine tree too before we both got serious
and put our hats on, me with a Lindy, both ears
covered in flaps, she with a rag, a kind of
bandage, and referenced Job and Jeremiah
and I said "Perish the day" but didn't mean it
for I was lucky, I said so once, and I did
swaying, the pine tree too, though maybe
she swayed first, stunted as she was,
but don't worry, I won't be struck dead
for my poetry, I'm too old for that,
and if I'm too loud it's all about the things
I'm trying to find the word for—murder, greed—
a single word, contamination, scandal,
moaning—though that's personal—even swaying, even
if I'm surrounded by others, even if I
caress the suffering branches, for I have permission.

Hell

JONES & LAUGHLIN

It was easy to call it that because of the
smoke pouring through the bricks or just the
bricks themselves burning and we kept picking up red-hot
chunks and where we could we reinforced
the outer walls above and below our heads,
and who and what we were we couldn't exactly
tell for we were covered in soot and hopped
away from the heat like hot dancers
for we were creating flames for those on the mountain
who drove up the steep sides to see the view
and took their visitors with them so they could express
their gratitude, though no one up there knew
that we wore thick white Tom Mix gloves with the word
"diamond" imprinted on the cuff and a large
red star as if on the knuckles and we were juggling
the burning bricks and our hands were blistered
and after a while our thick black shoes were steaming,
talk about inner and outer circles, talk about
Virgil whose name was something from Eastern
Europe near the Carpathians, soup out of cabbage,
meat out of fat, garlic from dog-star roses.

Mule

What good did it do him to sit in the white tub
and soap his back with a curved brush? He was
a mule who circled around the monstrous stone
from right to left, dragging and grinding and wearing
the blinders, and one time he tossed the hay
over his head and turned his teeth to one side
to catch it the way a mule does, bending to eat
the sweet and tasty grasses, and that's when a stick
of sorts was used to guide him; you should have seen him
weighing tomatoes, in spite of the welts,
you should have seen him unloading bituminous coal
with a long shovel, pushing it down the chute
the way he and his kind did every winter
for twenty-five cents a load, give or take some.

Wilderness

Given how deer are pests now
you'd think it was no big thing watching one
run up Union Street at six in the morning
in the middle of town looking for a woods
though he may have smelled the river, which only confused him—
at least that's what I think—and he turned right
on Jefferson toward the hills, if you consider
the corner where an impatient woman was running
in place and we went softly in different directions
for we were too ashamed to look at each other.

Not Me

It wasn't me but someone else in his eighties
sitting against a wall and it had to be
his mother sitting beside him well over a hundred
and maybe blind—I couldn't tell—and feeding her
from a tin plate or maybe it was foil
of some kind—I don't remember and when
a small girl maybe three or four came by
in tan stockings with horizontal blue stripes
and new blue shoes—and sunglasses I remember—
it could have been Crete—Heraklion, I'm sure of it
he stared in disbelief, maybe in envy,
maybe even in joy, and turned to his mother
to whisper something and folded his stiff fingers
over his belly and broke out into a smile
and half closed his eyes and almost nodded,
there were so many decades between them—
he could have slapped the ground with gratitude.

After Ritsos

One man stood apart and announced to the others
it was a form of hysteria and explained
to them the roots and connections to a woman's body.

But it was only when they brought the donkey over
to comfort her that she stopped her screaming
and gradually turned to sobbing in response to
which a dozen handkerchiefs appeared,
and everyone explained things to his neighbor
but the donkey loved her more than the man did,
he who was looking for a tree to rub against.

And there was an unearthly sound he made
as he backed up against a wooden post
to ease the sores on his haunches,
and I was remembering my own donkeys
and the kindness of Anne Marie.

After the Church Reading Against the War

It was Galway kept talking about the sidewalk
and how it was made of stone and not cement
and what a great wonder it was to him,
but there was old snow piled up and I had to
walk in the street against the cars mostly
speeding cabs and I would have stood my ground
if someone there didn't pull me away although
what I remember I jumped over a barrier—
I sort of flew—and my pride knew no
bounds but at the restaurant I was too quiet
and maybe they thought I hurt my back or I was
thinking of death but I had probably
zeroed in on nothing, which no one can stand;

and it was such a pleasure driving home
with the window open and the smell of
winter on Route 78 and thinking
again of Galway and his stone sidewalk
and how I flew and how a bird ascends
at the last minute just to tease you, especially
crows, especially pigeons—and sparrows—so hungry
they stay for the bread and only when you reach down
do they go for the blue, and though it wasn't blue that night
but black, with snowflakes falling on your eyelids,
and though you did the bread later you flew
first over a red plastic fence, then over a wooden
and if there was only a starter wind to lift you
you might have never stopped flying, you might have *risen.*

112th Street (1980)

Where there used to be a telephone booth here
that's where she stood banging on the glass
wearing only a raincoat over her slip
accusing him of calling another woman
when he was only halfway out the door
and he was embarrassed when he recovered from
the shock and he tried to protect her from the shame
and couldn't believe her rage and how her eyes
flashed as if in a drugstore novel and he
embraced her while she covered her face with her hands
and he remembered it thirty years later with something
like shame himself—though they both laughed later—
but something was lost, especially when he walked
by the building where the phone booth used to be,
and she would suffer bouts of sickness and death,
quick and unexpected and obdurate—
what they never dreamed about—fighting
each other two hundred feet over the river.

Free Lunch

I don't give a damn who gets a free lunch
in the first Methodist church on Union Street,
I just wish they'd fix their roof and let us
alone for a while, though you can tell a *schnorrer*
because he looks around and then puts
two quarters in the jar instead of say
a sawbuck and looks so happy leaving
as if he'd just put one over on the canary
or the wild volunteer in the orange apron, but your
heart would go out to the large-headed woman
who picked up her doll from a wooden high chair
and carried it out September 11, 2012.

And for God's sake, someone bring up Isaiah
who had his faults amen but
refused to budge and he was sawn in half
at the end and someone bring up Debs
who ran for president five times
on the Socialist ticket and the last time
got a million write-in votes while serving
time because he hated war and said that
while there's a lower class, he was in it,
and while there's a soul in prison, he was not free,
and so on, so where's his stamp, post office?

Maryanne

Everyone gets her day, Maryanne whom I
talked to exactly thirteen months ago
it seems was more at peace than anyone else
and though she had twenty-three cats and lived in rural
Arkansas I remember her curled up
as we say and reading old Cambodian novels
on the sixth floor—I think it was—while Howard
raged here and there and I am grateful we got
back in touch after fifty-five years and I am
amazed they lived together again, he with his
castle in Burgundy and his young French wife,
she with her puffed-up eyes and her black dresses
though both of their phones are dead now.

What Brings Me Here?

Here I am again and what brings me here
to the same wooden bench
preaching to the city of Lambertville
surrounded by mayapples?

For who in the hell is going to lie down with whom in the hell,
either inside or outside? And you know it's amazing
to watch flies lie down with feces
or mosquitoes lie down with blue bloods
and over there is a double house you call a twin
and when the one on the right burned down in under a minute
the one on the left refused to budge, not even an inch.

I'm not saying a French horn with a trombone
or a fleabane with a fleabane

or in one case
wood as fuel with wood as a god.

And I'm not saying it doesn't matter,
grinding the faces of the poor,
or whether it's a song or not.

Even if someone got carried away
and swam across the East River to Little Poland;

even if someone called himself a remnant
and lay there for sale cheap in the cheapo bin

whose grandfather had a trumpet for an ear
and raged against the heartless
then lost his polished head lying down with the sycamores.

Durante

How could I ever lie down like that
listening to Jimmy Durante singing "Try a Little Tenderness"?
Wasn't there a war on and weren't legs being sawn off
by second lieutenants right out of medical schools
in Pittsburgh and Philadelphia, home of Montefiore (in one case)
and Albert Einstein North and Albert Einstein South (in the other)?
and wasn't my back getting tired carrying so much in
and out including celery and Raisin Bran and Eight O'Clock
and once a sofa and twice an upright piano and
wallboard out of my open trunk my body bent
forward a little and my elbows taking the weight, my
neck itself the telltale repository
of a hundred different pains, each one
enough to slow a gorilla down; and I should
love the mattress itself, which I have been sleeping on
for thirty-three years and I should have fixed the record player
and I shouldn't have put the box of records on the curb
and lose the voices that way, and I should have paid
a sixteen-year-old to lift my end of the piano
and I shouldn't have been so arrogant carrying
all alone a 4-by-8¾-inch wallboard
and I should have played patty-cake with the gorilla
and I should have let Louise carry her own sofa
or I could have carried the two cushions
and put them back in place on the open porch
waiting for the truck to park in the flower bed.

The World We Should Have Stayed In

The clothes, the food, the nickel-coated iron
flower tables, the glass-and-wood-fluted doorknob
but most of all the baby girls holding
chicks in one arm and grapes in the other
just before the murder of the Gypsies
under Tiso the priest, Slovak, Roman Catholic,
no cousin to Andy, he Carpatho-Russian
or most of all Peter Oresick, he of Ford City,
he of Highland Park and East Liberty
Carpatho-Russian too, or just Ruthenian,
me staring at a coconut tree, I swear it,
listening late on a Saturday afternoon
a few weeks before my 88th to
airplane after airplane and reading the trailers
by the underwater lights of yon organ-shaped
squid-squirming blue and land-lost swimming pool
the noise a kind of roar when they got close
I'm watching from the fifth floor up, Warholian
here and there oh mostly on the elevator but
certainly by the pool, his European relatives
basking under his long serrated leaves
coconuts near the top—ripe and dangerous—
like Peter, coming from one of the villages inside
Pittsburgh, like me, half eastern Poland, half southern
Ukraine, born in the Hill, on Wylie Avenue,
the first village east of downtown Pittsburgh,
Logan Street, the steepest street in the Hill,
two blocks—at least—a string of small stores and
Jewish restaurants, Caplan's, Weinstein's, I was
born at the end of an era, I hung on with
my fingers then with my nails, Judith Vollmer's
family was Polish but they were twelve miles away from
Peter's village, this was a meal at Weinstein's:

chopped liver first or herring or eggs and onions, then
matzo-ball soup or noodle or knaidel, followed by
roast veal or boiled beef and horseradish
or roast chicken and vegetables, coleslaw
and Jewish pickles on the side and plates
of cookies and poppy-seed cakes and strudel,
Yiddish the lingua franca, tea in a glass,
the world we should have stayed in, for in America
you burn in one place, then you burn in another.

Divine Nothingness

I have to say I can't find the *Book of Brightness*
anywhere, not Amazon, not even the library at
Princeton, though I almost scream at the librarian
"it was carried across the border
from Provence into Spain and Portugal
and tied with hemp under the warm saddle
of the wisest donkey east and north of Madrid,"
and for herself I show her my ten fingers
and explain the separations and what the messages were
and how the years of baseball had interfered
through breakage and swelling now permanent and how
there are ten candles waiting to be lit
and what the permutations and distortions were
and how I wasn't crazy but had to find
the book to round out my education
and I was losing faith in Princeton, what with the
shoes and dresses in the windows and I could have
gotten in touch with the unfathomable
if only Princeton had it and I gave her the
title in Hebrew as well as a short lecture
and what came out of what but I had to go through
the glass doors with nothing but an egg sandwich
wrapped in plastic the way it used to be wrapped
in wax paper and either go down to Trenton
or figure out the permutations by myself
and I blamed Allen Ginsberg for all this
since I know they had the *Book of Pure Suffering*
written in the same century as *The Brightness*.

He Who Is Filthy

He who has a forehead
will have a forehead still,
and she who has a little brown egg
will have her nest and give her milk
in the most unlikely place of all;
and Johnny Cash will sit with his hand
on one leg and his other hand holding his head up,

and Learned Cohen will get on his knees
before his brilliant violinist;
and he who is filthy will be filthy still
and most of all, Thelonious Monk
will turn around again and again,
a different tic from mine
but equally respectable.

Lifewatch

Good to lie down in a yard of shadowing bimbo trees
against a dying redbud near a Japanese maple
whose deliquescent branches year by year
it gets darker and darker.

Good to be near a fence which unlike its neighbors
both up and down it's all of wire a see-through
chain-link different from the wooden walls,
the jails nearby, the swimming pools and sling chairs.

Good to be here finally filling in the gaps
and drinking coconut milk again
and out of debt forever.

from
Galaxy Love

Bio VIII

Refusing to listen to just any song that comes my way,
playing the mouth organ in homage to Stephen Foster,
soaking my big toe in memory of Libby, left foot,
and reading Hardy, all I ignored out of musical prejudice,
thinking seriously about the foothills north of Tampa, the Alps,
hating the thirty-five-story apartment buildings in South Beach,
always loving the fish sandwiches in Key Largo, the fishermen,
trying to get it straight about Stevens and Hemingway, who
     punched whom,
reading Ezra's chinoiserie for its gossip
thinking Jane Freilicher's eyes are like mine, only mine are browner
listening to Bach's Unaccompanied Suites, listening to "Helpless."

Hiphole

As far as the hiphole, every night I dug
into the dirt so I could put my body
partly underground on my long walk from
Lake Garda to Venice and thence to Bologna
and then third class to Florence, for the body
on either side can't rest on a flat surface,
say a wooden floor, but when we slept in
trees we must have slept facedown on top of
a branch and locked our hands to keep from falling
especially if we moved too much in our sleep
for we were monsters then and led alternative
lives with leopard skin of sorts and powerful
tails not to mention sharp teeth for cutting
and jaws for ripping and bird-like claws for holding
on and sometimes for piercing and sometimes just for
flea abatement or simply musing and scratching,
though we had holes too in the crowded forest
close to our trees, surrounded by our bushes,
for we lived mostly in the understories
and that way we left our lakes for distant cities
or what we took for cities then, the thought
was still with us when we were eating
mortadella and warm tomatoes and washing
our faces at the spigots stopping in
the Romanesques to look at the renderings;
we already knew the routes, we had our knapsacks
packed with toothbrushes, dictionaries, sweaters,
and Swiss knives, though we still walked on our knuckles.

Blue Particles

Don't ever think of Coney Island
where the rabbits once ran wild
or the afternoon we went swimming
though it was only May for we had graduated
and we spent the night eating hot dogs at Nathan's
and took the Screamer back to 96th Street.

Nor should you love too much the white pole
or the long and noisy ride through Brooklyn
the No. 2 that delivered you to your front door
and the Dutch freighter that delivered you to Antwerp,
then the Gare du Nord.

Nor your stubbornness every morning at the small table
and what it was like to walk out into the sunlight
and how the blue particles were your chief influence,
that and the Book of Isaiah
and King Lear rolling in the dirt on Chalk Mountain
the early part of your life.

Ghost

You could have stared all day
and it would rather get more radical than less
or more complex or more fragmental,
chaotic is what I would say,
a rabbit with its own rules,
its nose twitching maybe its ears
the last thing to go
the ears are the last thing to go
the gift of hearing

with no sign of life
neither heart nor lung
but the hearing remains
even if it's like an echo
a tunnel a hole where it goes the ghost goes.

Ich Bin Jude

Who was it threatened to murder
a streetcar full of fucking Nazis in Wien
when he was in the country only two hours
and watched the car empty
including the festooned conductor and the decorated motorman?

The rain wouldn't stop.
The cheapest place in Europe—
September, October, November, 1954.
Your darling city.

Azaleas

There isn't a bee swimming in milk
here, just a perfect recollection of the azaleas
at 23 York next door to the funeral parlor
and what the date was they appeared or when you
first discovered or rediscovered them was
and what their color was or what the word was
and what kind of insects inhabited them
and how the tourists were shocked by the beauty

and what the blessing is for azaleas I would have to ask
Rabbi Diana who has the thick books at her disposal
and I think understands the nature of endless gratitude
and whom I ask to plant something lowly on my hill
when the time comes and not to spend too long
on the Babylonian and to speak for me
and what I love and even to read this,
attested to May 11, 2014, Christian time.

Perish the Day

It's not just Larry who keeps going to
meetings when there's no one there—I went
to one in the latrine where a body was hanging
from a pipe and a finger had written in vapor
Just a Warning but whoever dragged him in
forgot to take his boots off before or after
and there was only one person there one live
person and he was cleaning the toilet with Ajax the magic
cleanser and he had an Irish accent mixed with
English I myself heard in Scotland
so that makes two when in walks Larry and then
for an hour or more he and Jonathan Swift, the
Ajax man, talked horses and, as Larry said,
an angel disguised as a fly flew into the ear
then into the brain of the horse, you should watch
where you put the swab and you should scratch the smooth skin
closest to the skull so your hand can slip
onto the horse's head which he would shake free
and move along the fence so he could bend down
for new weed and as for the meeting it lasted
just long enough to cut the dead man down and
wash him off but it was hard getting the boots
off without cutting or snipping for
there were no laces that's what I want to say
there were no laces on the day we unhanged him.

Poverty

Poverty I learned from the romance of my grandfather
coming over on steerage with three or was it six
dollars sewn into his vest and he ate
cheap and slept cheaper going from this bed to that and
by the time he was twenty he owned a string
of nickelodeons and at thirty he owned
the Mayflower Hotel in Atlantic City
plus the jitneys on Atlantic Avenue
but lost it all in the postwar depression
except he sewed a fifty-dollar bill
in his favorite vest and from this fresh start
he made a killing on Seventh Avenue
with a dollar bill in every right-hand pocket
the way there was a penny in penny loafers
and I put a twenty under my insole and
one time I had to tear my shoe apart
to pay for my supper the restaurant had the best
sweet potatoes anywhere my favorite vegetable
and Brussels sprouts my other and beets and cauliflower
but I had other shoes and found another
twenty and lived by a river with the birds
so loud in May I had to lock the doors
there were three and I had a table with
papers and dozens of books and sometimes
food and animal figurines, a small
wooden pelican, a glass rabbit, a
clay canary, and on a shelf a Deco
clock, a rooster and two pigs disguised
as salt and pepper shakers and some pots
I bought in Iowa and a photograph
of my parents in their store in Detroit, two
orphans almost in tears and in the next room
thirty-five books I am working with just now

and photos and dishes and manuscripts and candlesticks
and tin roses in a cloisonné vase
and more in the next room where I take my naps
and paintings and two thousand books upstairs
and boxes full of letters and rugs on the floor I
dragged from other continents and though I am rich now
by the old standards I always have a twenty
in one of my heels, usually the left foot and
usually underneath the insole I say
it's there for a rainy day I say it's just
in case I say it's for an emergency
though what it could buy now—not nearly enough
for a straw hat to cover my sunspots.

Bess, Zickel, Warhol, Arendt

Aunt Bess died from forgetting and when I
visited her at her last apartment she kept
asking me if I had eaten and poured
bowl after bowl of Rice Krispies for me though
I might add no banana, no milk
no sugar and most of all, no spoon.

And Zickel, my bewildered cousin, who suffered from
spinal curvature and dwarfism
both of which kept him in his small chair
in his little room down the hall and like the prophet
he was named for he fell down from his trances
and he was given to Utopian thinking
and lived by an old canal like the first one.

And there was a kind of Warholian laughter
which Andy and I used to resort to
walking across the Seventh Street Bridge
now the Warhol Bridge—the Allegheny River—
though there is no Gerald Stern Bridge anywhere
nor Michel Foucault nor Jacques Derrida.

And Hannah Arendt—I'm sure you remember her—
who went back to her lover her teacher in a
peasant's hut in the Black Forest and wept
in his arms as he in hers as he brushed the crumbs
from her Hebrew lips with his Nazi fingers
and published his last explanation in *Der Spiegel*
after his death in 1976.

Merwin

The way it was in the eighties
when we carried pockets full of quarters
to give to the destitute
and William ran a whole block south once
to give extra quarters because of the man's dog
a second giving for him
and it was his own Chow he mourned
for weeks on end and how
delighted he was—and shocked—
to see the Chow next door
with his characteristic blue tongue
and his proud and distant way
so that now in the time of no-age
that we share together though across
six hours of land
and six or more of water
I think of him writing in his room full of white light
as our friend Mary Ann describes it
where he's loading his pockets
and he will run down the best he can
to give a second time to the man
with the Border collie though it's more
like a third time now that I think of it.

Route 29

This is the place, isn't it?
I parked my car on the shoulder
and walked into the woods
thirty yards to the pool
of water the opposite side
of the canal and the river
the great maples and spruces
sometimes three feet deep
in the freestanding water.

And there is the stretch, isn't it,
where I told an astonished young policeman
I was a professor of police science
when he stopped me one night for weaving.

And this is the time of no-time
you get to know in your eighties
reading Paul Goodman and
studying the last poems of Duncan
identical to the typed manuscript
he inscribed for me as a gesture
of love in 1985
at the Pound conference in San Jose
where a door was flung open
in the room where the coats were hung.

Though the canary was red that time
and for a change his name wasn't Dickey
and he flew back into his cage
to get at the calcium,
he who loved horses
and died with his thin legs in the air
and was carried out secretly

to the 1938 Pontiac,
one of the many things
that disappeared around me
since those who first loved me have gone on without me.

Two Boats

I was eating half a chicken and keeping
my head away from the redbud branch that stoops
sometimes to poke me or just to caress me
as well as keeping the sun and wind away,
and sometimes I was Samuel Coleridge and sometimes
Oswald Spengler and I thought if we had
bought the houseboat in 1950 and started
up the Ohio, then down past Steubenville
to Cincinnati and the Mississippi,
how it all would have been radically different
for Donald and me, floating to New Orleans,
but his father never gave him the money and anyhow
he was too boring to live with for such a length
of time—I would have killed him—
                                and if Thanksgiving,
two years later in watery Sète, I had
closed a deal with the French sea captain
to rent a boat and cruise the Mediterranean
from Morocco on the left to Greece on the right
including Crete and Spain and Egypt, six of us,
all students at Montpellier, for what was then
a pittance, I think a thousand dollars a month
simple fare included, that makes a hundred
seventy dollars for each of us, the boat
was built I think when the Phoenicians
founded Carthage, the sail was red, a motor
was added for modernity—but we had our lives
to lead, or so we said, in four
or five cities, including school and jobs
and fiancées—but I have only a drop of
regret, the size of a raindrop that barely escapes
my redbud leaves, I sometimes shake them

to have a little drink, and I have abandoned
Spengler a hundred years ago and now it's
pauvre Spinoza again, he goes with my chicken.

Silence

I once planned a room for pure silence
the walls two feet thick
where I could listen to the Quartets
or just the loose notes floating by.

But I never minded the sound
of Stanley's cornet
mixed as it was
with the sound of the wind
and the shrieks of small birds
blown about over the water.

He, Stan, who stood on his front porch
facing the river
and blasted away at the black locusts
living there.

He—Stan—who borrowed my rowboat
to get a little exercise before he died
just after his displacement and heart attack
and just before Flo's breakdown and suicide.

For he was a D.P. American style,
his retirement stolen one day,
the owner in a cloud somewhere
and twenty-six years of work—
steel for Yankee Stadium and Verrazzano Bridge—
gone overnight,

his '53 Dodge truck in the backyard
with its hood up
just like his gold-laden mouth stood open in disbelief,
the grass growing up foot by foot in the dirt around him

for which I added two coats of green wall paint
whose purpose it was to create another layer
of foolproof sound intervention
to keep the grief out.

A Walk Back from the Restaurant

How fitting it was to see a fat and evil cat
in the dirt and dead leaves of a cement pot
next door to the Presbyters, the same self-righteous
bastards that moved dear Robbie Burns in his
modest apologia, "Holy Willie's Prayer,"
the single best poem of 1785,
and try to figure out which century the wood trim
and railings and such were last painted
and who the old woman was who lived there with her twenty cats
and how many years ago her loving husband died in his sleep
and how—and if at all—it was possible to disentangle
we'd have to probe the ultimate secret again
since the in-your-face and self-congratulating mayor
couldn't, in spite of his bulk and his slanted forehead, help us with that.

The Year of Everything

It was while he was collapsing under the weight of
the chifforobe that he considered inner and outer things
though at the moment inner was his pain and outer was
him at the other end in addition to the chifforobe itself.

He used to think of balance, harmony it could be
called, with maybe a slight tilt inward as if he were
moving his mind east ah gradually and even considering
the lotus and some straw to sleep on instead of the hairy

mattress and spring and headboard it would be impossible
to carry up Iron Mountain or Black or Red or Ragged,
whatever his fancy was and wherever his harmony took him,
and, as he said to his green Honda, it was only the body of Bliss he was

after, never mind "body," never mind that "bliss," a word
too close to happiness, ecstasy, something either
vague or unearned, though he at last had grown fearless
when it comes to languor and even provoked himself

as he did here with philosophical debate and a kind of
wordage he would have called too discursive when
he was twenty-five or thirty but he did what he did
and he praised the year he wrote his new book of poems

even if it was a year of murder and ignorance
talk about outer things, talk about the world
as opposed to the self and the name he gave
it was the year of everything.

Two Things

Always it's putting two things together
that don't necessarily belong there,
Dizzy Dean of the St. Louis Cardinals
calling in his outfield and striking out
the last three Pittsburgh Pirates to win
a crucial game at Forbes Field—and the
bombing of Addis Ababa by Count Ciano
the son-in-law of Benito Mussolini
who described the destruction in terms of lovely blossoms
spreading out in the smoke of the lower atmosphere.

The year was 1936 and my father,
driving a 1935 silver-gray Pontiac,
described the Ethiopians sitting on the heads
of African elephants, carrying poisonous spears
which would destroy the Fascists using outmoded weapons
from World War I too terrified to do battle
with Ethiopia—Abyssinia it was called,
a great empire which had resisted Mohammed
and *his* son-in-law 1,500 years earlier
and everything before and after since Sheba.

I also have a vague memory of the hood ornament
I think it was an Indian "chieftain"
with a dour puss as it was on old nickels
as I remember, and for all I know there's a stamp
with a feather or two, most likely turkey
but it could be goose or even crow but never
canary and never for that matter parrot,
so accurate the artists at GM were
whether they were designing the hood ornaments
of Chevys or Cadillacs, which I also remember,

for without knowing it I was an expert on many things
especially baseball cards and stamps and I had one of
Honus Wagner and a few gorgeous French Empires
which surpassed I thought those of the English since
if the sun never set on the British Empire
it did set on their artisans at least when it came to
stamps, it was a Martinique
I especially loved, the upright tits
and—in spite of the gender—the bolo knife that cut
its way through the forests as if the trees were butter

which brings up the great subject and what
an eleven-year-old was doing admiring tits,
especially the pointed kind that began
higher on the upper body than nature
allowed maybe with a tiny baby sucking
or one on her mother's back too small anatomically
all of which got him started at an early age
hunting through magazines for undressed women
and trading in flutter-books, his favorite the goings-on
between Bluto and Olive, Wimpy and Geezil watching

I could compare to flying the friendly skies
of newnited with a hit on cattle cars and a
boughten sandwich, this way bringing together
what doesn't at first (and second) blush belong there
which you might call a metaphoric rage
for we are used to that where like is more and
I have a pen with an eraser my darling
and you are a 1940 radio and
you are seventeen inches of snow in Michigan
shall I compare thee to a winter's day?

Larry

He kept a hog in Utah
as big as an old bathroom
and parked it in his parlor
so he could polish one bristle at a time

and he kept a horse in his heart
a capacious meadow surrounding him,
the one with a holy ankle,
nor did he forget the bruised jockey.

And he missed my war
though he had a good one of his own
for which he wrote the best poem known
of the alphabetized corpses

and suffered Ike only as a boy
and never took the ride
to Sète on a French bicycle
and staggered back home in the French moonlight.

I had the great honor of introducing him to New Orleans
and watching him jump with joy oh literally
as we visited Hebrew Rest for sorrow
and the caves on Bourbon for cold beer

and we both loved the same woman years apart,
and it was I who called her up
to give her the bad news to which she said
"Now I'm going upstairs to read every word he ever wrote."

Sunset

At the horizon line there was a touch of pink
but everything above was a heavy gray with
streaks of white behind it though yesterday it
was two black lines stretching across the sky with
the red then the pink behind it but it wasn't the
end of days, it was just two variations
showing through the slightly moving palm trees

but I wasn't sure that a madman wouldn't ride down the
street on a large white horse with a sword hanging
from his mouth murdering left and right with ten
million angels shouting after him or twenty
million monkeys as the sages of India have it,
all with harmonicas and pocketknives loving
Apocalypse, as they called it, given the darkness.

Orson

Orson Welles has been my philosopher
for the last few weeks now and if he's just a
phenomenon and doesn't really have a system
as Spinoza did or Anaxagorus, he
at least is consistent even if some of the things
he talks about are immensely unimportant
except to actors maybe or gossipmongers.

It was 1950—I think—in a Protestant church
near the Pont d'Austerlitz we met him directing
a small troupe in *Macbeth* even before he
made the movie; he was taking a vacation
from America during the naming of names and I had
the honor not only of watching them rehearse
but having some *vin ordinaire* afterwards.

Of the poets, it was Dylan Thomas he seemed to
love the most and just because I could speak
one poem after another he assumed
I was a tub-thumper myself though it was Stevens—
an English edition—and Hopkins I carried around
and hateful Pound I dragged from place to place
and Crane, his ecstasy.

As far as God
Orson, like every secularist, was evasive
and spoke of unknown gases and random objects
floating through the universe and called what was called
sin just selfishness—this from a heavyweight
eating his steaks and potatoes at 2 or 3 a.m.
the No. 1 saint of the sinners of old Hollywood.

Gelato

The two nuns I saw I urged them to
convert to Luther or better yet to join
the Unitarians, and the Jews I
encountered to think seriously about
Jesus, especially the Lubavitchers,
and I interrupted the sewer workers
digging up dirt to ask them
how many spoonfuls of sugar they
put in their coffee and the runners in
their red silk to warn them about
the fake fruit in their yogurt since
to begin with I was in such a good
mood this morning waiting patiently
for the two young poets driving over from
Jersey City to talk about the late forties
and what they were to me when I was their age and
we turned to Chinese poetry and Kenneth Rexroth's
Hundred Poems and ended up
talking about the Bollingen and Pound's
stupid admiration of Mussolini
and how our main poets were on the right
politically—most of them—unlike the European
and South American and we climbed some steps
into a restaurant I knew to buy gelato
and since we were poets we went by the names,
instead of the tastes and colors—and I stopped talking
and froze beside a small tree since I was
older than Pound was when he went silent
and kissed Ginsberg, a cousin to the Rothschilds,
who had the key to the ghetto in his pocket,
one box over and two rows up, he told me.

Ancient Chinese Egg

I counted wrong in the other poem,
it was five hundred years, not a thousand
so that meant the egg was cooked
during the time of Ben Jonson, it also
was neither simmered nor steamed, but baked
in the sun on the heated rocks, I'd say three minutes
in the way we keep time in this era and since I
"obtained" it in 1970 it had to be
the grandson, and the poets were late Ming
and one of them wrote about the swarm of flies
on his sick horse and what the smell of blood was
and one of them wrote about his *pauvre* hut in the mountains
as if it were still early T'ang but what the hell,
a hut is a hut be it this be it that
and self-pity in terms of the geese coming north
is the same both here and there, the egg on the outside
was perfect though I'm a little nervosa
of what I'd find inside so I tossed it
from hand to hand stopping once or twice
to read and reread the certificate
of priceless possession and how I could reduce
the value to zero by just two gulps,
or a few nibbles at the parameters;
ah, one of them wrote of his life
wasted on Weights and Measures and how his shoes
were ruined by the time he got home for he couldn't carry
them swinging from side to side
while he walked barefoot the thousand miles
for he was too old and soft and had a wattle
under his chin—he'd have to stop
dozens of times,
and consider that though the Manchu regime was coming,
in Europe it was no better

though since it was almost June he still could be saved
by the tragic solitary dark red iris
forcing its way again through the dense green hedges.

Loneliness

Nothing by or for itself, the sound of.
eggs hard-boiling in the hot water
echoed by the heavy rain that pours
down the broken spout, the cowardly lion's
roar answered by the moos of the buffalo
the bloody mouth of the one
by the sharp and polished horns of the other,
even Nelson Eddy
could hear someone else singing in his bathtub
the songs from his dumb movies

though when I once drove up the vertical highway
in Colorado to visit Elaine the Gnostic
and take her to the stone mountain
where her husband fell
we drove back without talking
though she touched my knee in gratitude and when
we reached the very top there were no trees
only flowers grew there
accompanied by nothing
the name of which was loneliness
which Shelley the poet himself suffered from
among his beleaguered women
you'll die remembering.

Hamlet Naked

It was a theater west on 47th
that smelled inside of urine
both upstairs and down,
you wouldn't believe it
but it was *Hamlet* naked, not *Lear*, not love
next door to where ten or so men
were facing the walls and swaying
in what was called a bookstore
across the street from Nedick's, orange soda and hot dogs
for which I'll say just this
that some could bend their knees while swaying
and move their lips
and shut their books with a loud amen.

When I walked east past Broadway
I hesitated too long and by this act
I had to press the button twice to change
the red to green, for I was in a fog,
and someone should light a bonfire
since I could walk wherever I wanted then
and didn't know north from south or east from west
nor was it Papp *his* Hamlet circa
1968 nor Dante naked nor Faust,
it was instead your normal lewdness
posing in a halfhearted way as art.

I was ironic then as I am now
but my head was too far down as if I were looking
for nickels, though anything less than a quarter
I wouldn't disgrace myself.
Maybe I was looking at the metal doors
open to let the light down into the cellar,
Gregory Corso playing the harmonica,

Diana Trilling with a toy cello,
both I saw one day on Avenue A
among the bags of rice and the boxes of lettuce,
the old Ukrainian restaurant which this late date
could be an expensive Armenian or Ethiopian,
diners sucking it up with chunks of bread
for there is nothing but improvement now
among the lettered streets, and there was a learned
couple with a five-year-old, all three had
matching neckties—I want to wear one
when I go into the cellar, I want to be
arrested for causing havoc, especially when a
crowd gathers around the opening—
in New York a crowd can form in a second, think
of Gregory, a blue jay on his head,
think of Diana seeing a live rat,
think of me lying on the gunnysacks
               my left arm up
               conducting.

Fall 1960

Castro himself—you won't believe it—ate Wheaties
for breakfast at his hotel in Harlem
I remember it was the Theresa and they
cooked chickens in the kitchen they brought over
from Cuba for they were afraid John Foster Dulles
or his brother Allen Dulles might poison them
and Khrushchev took off his heavy black shoe and turned on
the radio at 4:45 to hear the
latest adventure of Jack Armstrong, the All-
American Boy and I even stopped
kissing my close friend's wife while he was in the bathtub
soaking, drunk and singing songs from the islands
off Messina, he who worked for the Quakers
and was fired for drinking and singing, though soaking
was acceptable, here is the song:
    We the Piper Hudson High boys
    show them how we stand,
    never tired of Wheaties,
    the best food in the land
    so won't you try Wheaties
    the best breakfast food in the land.

Skylark

That's my suit Johnny Mercer is wearing,
the buttonhole at top visible through the lapel,
the jacket loose the hands falling
naturally in the trouser pockets,
the look required one of disdain what you'd call
arrogance for want of a better word,
a joke Hoagy Carmichael told him
still in his smile, the words to "Skylark"
in his inside breast coat pocket,
honeysuckle everywhere, everywhere,
the main lie of the thirties and forties, the last
century, the one I was born in.

The Other

I woke up determined to turn everything
upside down, to convert music to protest
and protest to song,

always struggling against the Other

and there was a baby robin on the ground
screaming just to unnerve me and—
more—there was its mother in the Japanese
maple half-scolding, half-beseeching,
all this to bring me to my knees
to unhold myself from the screwed-in two-by-four
where I was doing one leg at a time to strengthen
my back and stomach muscles and I discovered
again the Other could be the mother or the
baby, or even the tree itself.

New Poems

The Camargue

The rain came down for hours
unlike the fitful showers of eastern America
under the awnings and the doorways waiting;
the hail was the size of hardballs
denting the roof of our rented Renault,
the size of softballs, the size of mushballs,
the size of small white horses running through
the lavender, their bodies soaked, screaming
eagles the size of lead quarters,
the *New York Times* the only rain hat I ever had:
you fold and crease it, it's worth three dollars, four dollars,
nobody wears a newspaper hat now
everyone wore a newspaper hat then.

Red and Swollen

In the museum of thumbs there was one red
and swollen that had almost flattened out by
pressing the metal scale constantly while the
mouth moved differently asking questions and chewing on
nothing, as if to distract you, as if to
assure you there was swollen love in his heart and
once you got the hang of it you realized
there were other brutal thumbs, and that the
museum was full of our red and swollen history
and what you said was the butcher in the old
A&P on State Street in Trenton but what it was
was really Lockheed Martin in Maryland hard by the Pentagon.

Baby Rat

for LUKAS MUSHER AND MELINA GIAKOUMIS

A blind baby rat Luke and Melina tell me
staggering, hopeless, alone, on a burning street
near Columbia, maybe on Amsterdam,
north of St. John's, his two eyes empty
the sockets a dirty red, either born that
way or plucked out by a hungry
crow, the eyeball the crow's first delight,
the sweet and slippery taste thereof; someone
will kick the baby rat into a sewer
or pick him up with a tissue and throw him back
and get on his phone in a second to rid himself
somehow of the horrible sight, and I who
for two days now was thinking of the redwoods
and our walk in Muir Woods in the 1970s
thought of placing him in one of the upper villages
three hundred feet in the air protected by
maybe a spider's web, maybe
a few odd twigs, guaranteed
at least an hour of peace
for I have the privilege now
which I didn't have forty, fifty years ago
looking up and almost toppling over.

The Cost of Love

If I had to I could have banged my head
on the mud-packed walls of my underground office
and maybe get a gash or two from the crystals
either on my oversized forehead or my cheekbones
for that is the cost of love I have been adding
up in the red, the one on the right, it's tricky to
do a balance isn't it? For values are
hard to measure and I didn't read the book
of pain—I say enough of pain, and down with
666—I'll take kindness, most of all
kindness, for love is the murdered thing.

Hearts Amiss

How wrong it was to look at those hearts incised
in maples and birches with a loving
arrow between them, especially when the tree
grew larger and the hearts expanded
the way they do, and love took over the tree
and we said, "Here's another," and our own hearts
broke in two with envy and regret,
but what we didn't know then was they were emblems,
signs, of something deeper and more discordant
for they—the lovers—had turned to sacrifice
and torn the other's heart out from its moorings
and held the wet organ in their own hands,
loose and disconnected from the strings,
the hearts of lovers deeply separated
from what were once such arrows of desire,
and some were painted red on buried stones
planted in the ground like broken teeth.

Hebrish

At the confluence of tea roses and Russian sage
we made a right at the curved iron fence,
one of my dead friends beside me explaining how trees communicated
but I couldn't understand a thing because it was all blurry—
the way it gets—and though I knew him well
I couldn't say for sure now whether it was Larry or
Phil or Galway or Charlie until I realized it was me
talking in some kind of Hebrish they spoke
in my town by the Delaware and it was used
for code the way one of the Amerindian languages
was used in World War II the Germans couldn't in a
million years break since they weren't as pragmatic
irrational and in-your-face as the English and Americans were.

I noticed the bees were digging in for a late lunch
of what for them was boiled beef and horseradish
or maybe it was just for me, and they were bent over
guzzling madly while paying no attention to the two
of us or in anyway tired of the nectars since it
ran the whole gamut from oysters to soup to—well—
boiled beef to strawberry-rhubarb pie
and a little whiskey after, some of it spilled on the
vanilla ice cream that underlay the pie it had once overlaid,
all of this depending on the blossoms they circled over
and bent down upon, a cafeteria as good as the one
on Broadway called Stanley's I circled and bent over
expending nickels dimes and quarters when the Dulles brothers
ran the country.

                                    It was Larry, I'm sure now,
and what we talked about was cardboard
and we were amazed that in the open spaces
beside the hotel on 47th Street

there were four or five small cardboard "houses,"
both of us remembered,
the homeless had claimed to sleep in and provide
a safe place for their black plastic garbage bags,
the size of a room at the Sloane House on 34th Street
near Pennsylvania Station where I put up
the price of a meal then for a clean pillowcase
with little or no stuffing and a cardboard
bed as stiff as metal and a cardboard
breakfast of cardboard bread and eggs and between us
we talked cardboard, shirts from the cleaners with sheets of
cardboard we drew on, cardboard soles in ruined shoes
we both wore when we were children, cardboard hats,
cardboard to lie on listening to outdoor concerts
and cardboard masks we made with scissors and crayon
for costume dances, Balls is what we called them
as if we were art students in Paris about to
swim in the nearest fountain.

                                        Though what I want to
say is the bees were too busy to do us any
harm and it was packs of wild dogs, not swarms
of bees, that terrified me (Larry too) except for one
occasion when I pushed the wrong end of an old
broom into a hive of yellow jackets on the underside
of a low-lying garage roof and an angry swarm chased
me through the yard and over a fence, hating
any form of criminal intrusion, urban renewal or
gentrification, I who couldn't resist intrusions,
who never could, omnivorous as I was, living on
apples and bananas as well as baby lamb chops,
who ran like hell that day (Larry too)
for we in our separate ways didn't want to be
paralyzed then eaten by larvae, none of us dead ones did.

Cherries

I was waiting to try out one of my inventions
from the flattop garage roof—parachutes this time—
when I tasted a black cherry from the next yard,
wondering even at that age
who had prior rights and what was constitutional,
so instead of jumping I wrote a brief brief
called Yaakov vs. the Tree Trunk
where everyone laughed herself crazy
at Marlboro vs. Madison
or Red Stain vs. the State of New Jersey,
so bless me you fools
for aren't you mortals?
and don't you bend your body down
over the water to taste the ice?
and who, in your family,
even ever just thought of
swallowing a goldfish from the bowl,
say, picking up its slippery body,
bending your neck back and gulping it down
even before they entered law school.

No Kissing There

It wasn't only Eleanor I kissed
but de Beauvoir with her net bag
on the Street of the Butchers,
and I would have made it Red Emma
if I were a little older and Mary Shelley
a century before, I was so prone to
kissing, and I kissed in this life, on her mouth,
Meryl Streep who stopped at my boughten table,
and when did it start, this kissing?
and when did kissing itself start?
And was it the nose or the mouth?
Let's name children, grandchildren, dogs,
books, lovers, wives, friends,
and don't forget kissing the air
in Rome and Buenos Aires to show your distance

and don't forget kissing your teachers who
taught you one thing through neglect and abuse

and don't forget Rilke's simplistic separation
of life and art, no kissing there.

Lake Country

We were either fighting against time
or not paying any attention to it
and one of us was upstairs in the back bedroom
sleeping with one hand on the cold floorboards
or it was the knuckles thereof and
one of us was in the kitchen making coffee and
arguing against Artaud's unfair reading
of "The Ancient Mariner" and insisting it was his madness
got in the way or maybe it was just that he was
French and misunderstood English poetry,
continuing, as he did, the absurdity of Poe's
genius, somewhat in the same fog-ridden craziness
as the lore of Jerry Lewis,
that ridiculous freak with the gooney
voice at last growing old,
and though the coffee brewer protested Poe
wasn't a poet the way Stevens was, or Frost,
he still remembered exactly where and when
Artaud refused to include him
in his anthology though he did include Mussolini,
and we all decided to drive down to Philadelphia
for liverwurst and onion sandwiches at the Olney Diner,
somebody's birthday, one of the calamities of the late fifties.

Wet Peach

He reached inside his chest for understanding,
where there was a loose heart attached by strings
that could be stretched and severed he could grab
and joggle, and wet as it was in his wet
hands, and (finally) holding it there in his palm
he almost moaned for he was thin-skinned to
an extreme and moved by the slow beating such
that he wore the strings on his sleeve that sometimes
drained in red on the rag he carried with him
for just that possibility or likelihood
and stuffed it like a peach in his side pocket.

March 17th

My song of the pea has me
and my wife carefully pouring
the packet of dry seeds
into the water holes,
the river on one side, the
canal on the other, the
soil perfect for early peas,
the wind scarring our bare ankles,
our thighs wracked with pain—
as it has me planting my walking stick
into the high ground and the roots taking hold,
and ripping it out when the first peas appear—
not to forget the great snow of the early nineties
the day after I bought two bicycles
to welcome in the spring,
the ice on the water a foot thick—
as it was in Boston on St. Patrick's Day
in an Irish bar lecturing my poor son
on potatoes and him trying to shut me up—
as it was—I remember—in Kansas State
a one-man show and a private showing
of Thomas Hart Benton's work, the docent
hinting at a certain closeness between her and
the master, the wife, as I recall
after his extensive travels throughout the state
only saying, "My husband is a great painter"—
the Russian sage smelling the same everywhere,
my fingers savoring the odor.

No House

Suddenly there was no house
but most important the hand-sewn curtains
were on the living-room windowsill facing the front porch
though they constantly presented a confusion
since at the same time all the windows
in the front room were already covered
with lace to add a certain stiffness
to accompany the formally placed
furniture: armchairs, cupboards, rugs, including
the one I carried across Crete, up a steep hill,
on a plane, a car, some steps, but Lord,
the rug on the second floor is the Greek one,
the Mexican rug is on the first floor
near Gershom Scholem and Ralph Waldo, the mind,
which I love above all things, is so sloppy.
In the meantime, the poet, whatever
his honors, always writes his new poems
in obscurity, he's always a beginner,
even if he's already living in his hut.

Mount Hope Cemetery

At last I'm taking the accusation
seriously and I'll surprise you
by singing José's song to Carmen
instead of the nostalgic crap I've been living on
I first heard at the ornate old opera house
in Rabelais's city in the South,
sitting in a box of faded velour chairs
meant for smaller people a bare three feet away
from the smugglers and card sharks
singing their hearts out, my very first opera
I never heard again even the two years
you bought season tickets to the Met
all of which should convince you to lie down beside me
thirty, thirty-five years from now
in the Jewish section of Mount Hope
on the bluff facing Grant Street
even though (as you say) you're not Jewish
and I would sing too much
and you're too young to die
and, anyhow, "I had a crush on the rabbi"
I sometimes ate lunch with, though it was Kabbalah
and its cousin Zen we talked about
in the years she lived my side of the river
where she is now buried in my favorite valley
above the small city where I first met her
and danced and sang a brucha across the street from—I think—
the People's Store almost at
the corner of Bridge and Union
where we often had a late lunch at Guiseppe's,
mostly minestrone or Greek salad,
she with her motorcycle, I with my bag of books,
she with her Gabirol, I with my dictionaries.

Red Jungle Fowl

Among the whatnots and the barnyard animals
in my small living room in Lambertville
there are two or three red jungle fowl
of beaten tin and bent iron
which we call chicken
in among the sofas and tables
which I'll call a fatted fowl,
in its own way like the fatted calf
we burned all night
while Moishe was negotiating on a mountain,
or so he said, with something invisible.

But the fowl and fowls like him
whether they are gods or not
and whether they're smeared with gold or not
are different from the young bulls we called calves
who were worshipped, you know, for their strength and courage,
so unlike *chickens* who are mean and cowardly,
eat anything, and scratch anyone's eyes out,
and though all fake gods shit,
not all are as brutal and ugly as they are.

And if you think the talk of sacrifice
is hardly relevant then just walk
through Jerusalem as I have
and listen to the crazies talk about another Temple
and high priests burning fat for the Name
and studying the plans of Ezekiel
as if they were at the drawing boards
at Caltech or MIT,
so many cubits for the inner and outer walls,
so many (Hebrew) feet for the high altar,
and for the sink you wash your hands in,

and parapets for drums of burning oil
and a small stage for the flute and one for the horns
and rows of straw shoes for cleanliness,
and in the back a kitchen for the priests
to have a little bite of fowl
and a silver cup for a schnapps
to drown it in.

And no woman in the inner court
and no woman anywhere in pants
or short skirts
or bare arms or shoulders,
and no cleavage
or low-cut jeans
belly buttons, bare feet,
hair, T-shirts,
breasts, thighs, ankles,
necks, lips, eyes,
or without an arm a leg or a head,
or shaved anywhere,
and butcher blocks with cedar-cladded openings
for razor-sharp knives to slice the necks
and cut the yellow skin off,
the best schmaltz money could buy
and the best cock-a-doodle you ever heard
mostly to warn the Arabs
who walk on the roof.

Knucklebones

Like Frida, who had a bellyful of nihilists
I had a bellyful too,
only it was hellfire ecstatics
riding, as they did, on white horses
with swords sticking out of their mouths.

I lived in Alabama PA
I loved the cheap real estate
but I hated that they drank white vinegar
and ate supper at five o'clock
and what their tattoos were and where they put them
so I gave up talking
and spent the afternoon in the low mountains
and drove up and down the steep roads
studying the cows.

Frida, full of charm and cunning,
asked Henry Ford if he was a Jew.
He loved to dance with her
nor did Rivera shoot him with the .38
he carried in his hip pocket
for he was driving the new roadster Ford gave him.

So here's to Miniver Cheevy and here's to Shelley
and here's to Charlemagne and here's to Trotsky
and Trilling's stockings and Adlai Stevenson's shoes
and Dorothy Day and C. K. Williams and Galway
and Jack Dempsey and Brest-Litovsk and horseflies
and herring salad and beetles and dead man's float
and the little man on the wedding cake
and the cake itself and
stuffing your mouth with sugar,
and here's to arthritic fingers and here's to knucklebones.

Frutta da Looma

Thinking if trees suffer pain from the cutting
there has to be blood as evidence except that
the wetness is not so often red and clotted
but something reflecting the color of the wood
itself, all of which brings me back to 1952
and the horrific contests between
big Al Brayson and myself with half the
school watching, our axes honed to a point,
sometimes him and sometimes me dropping our
tree first, and blood you might say in half of
Long Island among the pitch pines and maples,
mementos of the forests that extended from
Maine to the Upper Peninsula of Michigan,
pools of blood in the springtime flowing into
the Great Lakes or further west, the hemlocks,
the blood different it seemed from the huge white pines
though it took us a second great war to realize
that one good tree deserves another, even a
frog, for that matter, even a flower, even
a freight train, even a dress white frutta da looma.

Adonis

I forgave him the debt of having to explain
where he came from, who his angry father
and his loving mother were, or I relieved him
from any excuse and sat
dozens and dozens of years ago at the counter
of Zak's, Broadway and 103rd,
he on the other side, his sleeves rolled up,
his hands, his arms, in steaming water, washing
dishes and frying pans and talking music,
his dream of studying at Juilliard,
the tiny practice room a rich lady
from the Upper East or Upper West Side paid for,
listening all afternoon to him playing
the small piano, his large romantic gestures,
his hair wild, his hands and fingers amazing,
classic Polish; he was from Little Italy,
a high school dropout, me a graduate student
at Columbia, then I left for a year in Europe,
and when I came back I looked him up at Zak's,
the manager told me he was dead, no one
knew the facts, I thought of him
for years, I remember that we
took him out for dinner on Amsterdam
and he unspooled his dream again and told us
about the music he had written that week,
conducting with one hand, it was a loss
I couldn't recover from, I was awake
night after night but I can't even remember
his name, I lost it years ago, dear Shelley
this was Adonis too,
praise him.

Tony Was Right

Tony was right, I traveled by Greyhound bus
to New York City for seven dollars and was
a Jew of the entire world, what the Rooskies
called a Cosmopolitan, and slept in
many parks and on the ground in
France and Italy and washed at
public spigots and ate the warm tomatoes
and petted and kissed ferocious dogs, especially
near Padua, and stayed there day after day
to look at the Giottos and fainted
on the stone floor of a bank in Florence
after sleeping for two hours in the grasses of
the Boboli Gardens, and he is right, I opened
my window to yell at the rude truckers
forcing their way past cars at the entrance to tunnels
and bridges in New Jersey and I hope he remembers
our swim in the freezing water of a natural basin
carved over two million years ago in a huge
round stone at the top of a mountain
in Arizona we climbed all day to reach;
but bless him anyhow even if he doesn't
for he does remember how I sang "La Marseillaise"
and some hits from *La bohème.*
And God bless Eleanor Roosevelt. And God bless Erroll Garner.
And God bless Rosey Rowswell.

Blessed as We Were

As far as love
you know the favorite challenge she throws to he,
"What color are my eyes?" and watches him squirm
and hedge, and hedgitate, and argue and lie, and
yours are brown and by the way I love
everything about you—except a little—
for what if you praised, say, everything I wrote
without so much as the smallest reservation?
Speaking of which, in my poem "Larry" you
—and Ira as well—didn't recognize that "hog"
was the name for the huge motorcycles
that overweight and bearded veterans
ride up and down our highways sometimes
twenty or thirty, three abreast sometimes
in true formation, the size, as I said in the
poem, of a bathroom,
crowding out everything in the two small downstairs rooms
of the Utah house, and when I looked the word "hog" up
in my huge thesaurus there was no reference
to motorbike or motorcycle but there
was a reference when I looked up "motorbike"
to "pig," ah how polite and incorrect,
I never heard it called a pig, "Let's drive
our pigs up 611 into the mountains,
let's mount our pigs, hang onto the ears
for support when you're coasting downhill,"

and for the Iberian poet of the eleventh century,
Ibn Gabirol who wrote in Hebrew
but bought his food and ate in Arabic
whom I'll be leaving, or he'll be leaving me
for whom I write and whom I read,
and Ira and Phil and Muriel

and Galway and William and Charlie
and Levis here and Bishop there,
her "Gas Station," her "Moose,"
and Gershom Scholem and Benedictus Spinoza
and Judith and Michael and Mihaela and Jean Valentine
and Ross Gay and Joan Larkin and Jane Mead and Wackadoodle,
or Blake and Shelley or the Rooskies and Poles
and always the French and Spanish
and Roethke and Schwartz and Berryman and Goodman, all those,
and Eddie and Li-Young, both from Chicago,
and Toi from Hamtramck, her heart in New Orleans,
where I spent an afternoon with a nun once
discussing the prophets, Micah most of all,
"do justice, love mercy, walk humbly
before your God" whom the Gideons believed foretold
the greatest of Jewish healers turned into God,
as Isaiah foretold, they said, the Virgin Birth,
                              who taught English and Latin in a high school
in Minneapolis I think, and wore civvies,
a white silk blouse and a plaid skirt
and small heels, short stylish boots I think,
and had an understanding that I revered—
I'll call it knowledge—she reminded me of
Dorothy Day whose *Catholic Worker* I published
poems in, 1957, 1958; everyone
stubborn, disobedient, everyone loving
something greater than themselves
                              and, as you know, my favorite places
were the tiny shtetls, I'll call them that,
which sometimes were under bridges or over tunnels
with endless wooden steps and sometimes piles
of garbage, cigarette wrappers, crumpled
cans of beer that mercifully when the snow
covered them were seen as tiny hills, sometimes
held down by pebbles as gravestones nearby,
Polish and German, were also held down

to keep the dead from rising and coming back,
to have just one more cigarette and look
one more time at the FDRs on the wall
cut out from the aging pages of *Look* magazine,
the only piece of literature in my house
aside from a clasped and ivory-covered prayer book;

and how I loved meadows, I already wrote
of the one near Cook Forest by Route 80 I called
my "bitter personal heaven" among the clover and
daisies, I said, but in a more recent poem
I called them clover and cornflowers,
but I was probably wrong the second time, I know
it's the same meadow, a quiet, windless place;

and also the empty roads in Perry County
an hour north of Carlisle, Pennsylvania,
where I walked endlessly to pet the cows
who ate near the wire fences; and almost bought
an ancient house and land with a trout stream on it
and a covered bridge and four or five outbuildings
but lost it when the owner decided to move there
since the Plain People were building a pig farm
near her main property in Lancaster, PA.

But it was southern Spain I truly loved
where we lived, in the ten hundreds,
and that's where I want to live again
though I have to check with Anne Marie, she is
the spine of this book as Red Emma was of another
and Sylvia Stern a third, I ask it in the minor
key we sang together in Córdoba,
the Spaniards were not yet Spaniards
and they were building plowshares into swords
somewhere up north in what was called Europe,
but blessed as we were we didn't even know it.

The Beautiful

I never heard no
so I guess Jim Wright's ashes
are scattered among the tea roses
in Carl Schurz Park a few steps from our apartment,
and the East River was the beautiful Ohio
in the last years he spent
with Annie before his death.

My river was the Ohio too
but more like, it was the Monongahela
or someplace between the two rivers,
that and the Allegheny,
as they merged with the Beautiful
and went a distance north before it curved around
west then south and through filthy Weirton
and godforsaken Steubenville
on its way to the mother of rivers.

He told me he used to listen to
the Pirates' games so he knew the announcer, Rosey Rowswell,
but I doubt if he ever heard Bishop Beck
ask God to bless Rosey as well as
Mayor Scully and Councilman Wolk and Eleanor Roosevelt,
as he stood in front of his chorus of saints
with their blue evening gowns and violins
in the great church on Wylie Avenue,
a block away from where I was born.

Well, God bless Bishop Beck and
God bless Jim Wright too,
who is not, I say *not*, in Hell
for Hell is Martin's Ferry—he said so himself—
where he was baptized and maybe bar mitzvahed

as well in some absurd little synagogue
and his portion, as we say, was maybe John,
the 15th chapter: "No one has greater love
than to lay down his life for his friend,"
John, a Jew, like the others, goddamn.

Torn Coat

Look what it is to have forgotten
the torn coat of "Vecchia zimarra"
from Puccini's *La bohème* and to remember
the other coats from Mount Horeb on down,
and look what it is to give your own coat away,
three times now, and to walk shivering
in three different countries, oh tears
for the opportunity and tears for a horse,
all bone on a hillside without a blanket and
him laughing at me because there were no tears
left for a freezing gracehoper.

From Wackadoodle

If you grew rich, as you say, by finding
your sand dollars on the Pacific coast
near Seattle, I made a killing on the Jersey Shore
near Wildwood but who's to say who's the richest
and what does it matter anyway.

Anyhow, you saw yellow switchbroom and wild elk
and walked the silken sands beneath
the stippled underwings of a low-flying
osprey, and you engaged in small conversation
with a ponderous banana slug before you
went to the bank—and I only saw my once beloved
pitch pine forest from the Garden City Parkway before I turned left,
certainly south of the Atlantic City Expressway, beginning
as you know, near Philadelphia.

I don't know where you went with your cookies
but I ended up at Wells Fargo on Bridge Street
and argued with a teller about her cheating overlords
and refused her love altogether until she
admitted their evil ways, and out of respect for her silver cross,
made her listen to something out of Jesus,
exploited, low-paid, soon-to-be-fired innocent,
trying her best to abide by the bank motto,
"Your happiness is ours" or was it
"Our only wish is your happiness"
trapped behind her small piece of marble
inside her cage.

Forfor

In New York the Second Avenue Deli is on
First Avenue for Canaanites always like to
go east—and true north is mainly for Inuits—
and as for Wells Fargo the criminals in charge
don't go to jail for their crimes
but empty their pockets of a few crumpled bills
and some loose change which I only mention
for ages hence and where Stanley's Cafeteria was
it's a perfume store now, not that
onion bagels don't stink to high heaven,
and why shouldn't we have perfumes
that smell of pea soup or noodles
for my cat Geoffrey has changed his name to Jacob,
for a gerund is a gerund
and my cat Nimbus was run over by
the sickleman in a 1978
Chevy on Labor Day of the same year
for Carter was still president, even on Christmas,
and my daughter Rachael had a
small graveyard for all the cats we lost
and she still has cats—I think six—
in Trickle-Down Alabama, for it's now called Huntsville
and its greatest hero is the famous Nazi, Wernher von Braun,
for once a Nazi always a Nazi,
for once a Confederate too,
and the water in the Blacks Only fountain was delicious,
for most Ashkenazis are Canaanites and *fore*, as in golf,
means "I'm going forward,"
or "look out before me"
or "get the fuck out of the way"
and bless me, Father Divine,
for my son's friends said "whadayee whadayee"
for their fathers and uncles said "whadayee whadayee" too

for it's twilight on the trail
(and my voice is still,
please plant this heart of mine
underneath a lonesome pine
on a hill).
And as for Christopher Smart's cat Geoffrey
consider my cat Muriel
who rose from the dead
to say her say
for she was a lion
a leopard and a cheetah,
and what are all thy forfors for
if thou lov'st not me?

Elder Blues

How dumb it was to put my box of records
on the curb when I first moved here, for I was
mostly abandoning things for a fresh start—
I guess my sixth or seventh—depending on what
you include from my first abandonment

whatever junk or sentimentality there was
in that box it also contained the songs of
Muddy Waters, Skip James and the songs
we heard one night in Philadelphia,
John Hurt I think, it was the Walnut Street Theatre
or the downtown Y at the corner of Broad and Pine

and how I hung on to a torn shirt, a
faded photograph and a pair of leather boots
for my last abandonment, the shirt a Goodwill
from Neiman Marcus,
the boots my Georgia Loggers,
the photograph the one of me in Europe
including mustache, turtleneck, and a touch of
arrogance, I guess out of Les Deux Magots,
the café where Sartre held forth.
Elder blues, right?

Under Your Wing

for PAUL CELAN

Blue rolls over me
as it always did
even against my will
and I am leaning again
against one of the fake pillars
of the House of God
and later the House of Peace
House of Good Morning, House of Good Night
sitting on a red pipe
in the September sunlight
in my new wool suit
among the helpless and bored
a Clark bar in my pocket
part of the debris too
of *my* existence—
or would you prefer
the anguish I
carried from place to place
neatly folded and perfectly creased
in my small velvet bag?

Punching Holes

There's no right and wrong here
but I just want you to know that
Tu Fu in the eighth century
and two of my students in the twentieth
confounded fireflies with distant stars
whereas my first take was to conflate them
with the holy sparks buried in the physical,
a figure basic to southern French Kabbalah
though I see now that the star collusion
was more literal and mine more in the realm of Thought
and is more a stretch, even as it's nice to think
of the small insect as a part of Jewish mysticism.
Think of the bottle as containing everything.
Think of the lid and how we punctured the holes.
This had to be the first zoo, although there were no leopards.

Never

No sense burning the red ants
with your father's Zippo lighter
when the freezing weather will do it,
and both red and black will soon be curling
and freezing, your friends, your enemies,
as the Fahrenheit goes from 80 down to
28 overnight in a shift that amazes
the weather gurus in front of their maps.

It's better to sink with Ophelia
in her crown of weeds
singing, in my case, songs from the thirties
or better yet to lie down with Lear
on Chalk Mountain, repeating what the Galilean said
and give, if you can, your last dollar
to a good cause or a half an apple
to someone living on garbage

or lying down to sleep
on the steps of St. Patrick's
or the First Romanian Shul on Rivington
saying again and again
in your grandfather's language,
he of the greasy white curls,
never, never, never, never.

The Late Celan

The late Celan
eating God
eating Jews eating
flies eating
corpses eating mud
eating blood eating
paper eating
Kafka eating
das Schloss eating
Melina eating
the clock eating
the Germans eating
their supper in the square
essing and fressing
eating worms eating germs
eating ham eating flan,
eating Clarissa, pig of my heart
thanks to my love
and her darling son
thanks to Celan
thanks to August
thanks to May Day
not Labor Day
and white shoes
and the news
down with Ronald
down with Donald
down with priests
down with Cohens
down with tweets
and student loans

———

and what did he love
he loved the field mouse
and the lizard
he loved the snow
and the blizzard
and the breaststroke
the legs that scissored
and ah, the Seine
his death again
and he loved she
Ilana Shmueli
and Mandelshtam
and a cat named Lily
and she loved him
and sometimes they kissed

Friday cold noodles
Friday cold night
Shabbos dinner
by candlelight
who knew my gimp
all day Saturday
who knew my limp
a davening imp,
a demon, a wizard,
again the lizard
with bulging eyes
freezing to death
no surprise

how wounded he was
performing for Heidegger
a friend of Goebbels
John Skelton
an early rimester

I'm writing like
gefilte fish
Lake Erie pike
Mel Brooks
hotsy-totsy
a sick and brilliant Jewish poet
reading to a Nazi.

Warbler

The dead warbler started to sing
as she whom I love
bent down to pick him up with two reluctant fingers,
maybe the small finger (of the left hand)
curling, as at dinner,
and carry him home
and quietly put him
into a see-through plastic bag
as she did for salmon and roast chicken and pie.

I want to say "alas, poor warbler"
but warblers die too,
of disease, of age, of accidents,
as all birds do.

And like all birds
they sing when they're buried,
in this case in the freezer,
a cold graveyard,
two cartons of ice cream,
one vanilla, one dulce de leche,
to remember him by.

He was lifelike stiff and unapologetic
and he sang from time to time, dead or not,
a "rising trill," as the book says,
in the upper levels where the worms are.

At the Memorial of Al Dazzo, 1939–2017

for AL DAZZO AND *for* ROSS GAY

Weird the thing about fathers
Ross said to me,
the deacon said his father was talking to him
in Heaven by which he meant, we thought, *the* Father,
but maybe he did mean *his* father, the deacon's,
or maybe Al, *his* father,
who sold apples during the Depression,
in Brooklyn, I think, and I
seeing the crucifix on the wall, Jesus
in some kind of skirt, I said
"that is the craziest Jew of all," it was
the moment he cried his cry, the "father
why have you forsaken me," the 22nd
Psalm, first four words, before he drank
the sour wine, before he turned to smoke,
before he walked through fire, which purifies
as it destroys, it is that which nothing else
is so free as, that which is alive, and quick,
and quick, for where there's smoke there's fire
and where there's fire there's smoke
and where there's a shower, in Poland, there's a smokestack
and when there's IG Farbin there's Zyklon B,

and what about Heine—his "softly flows the *Rhine*"
became my soft the *Delaware* I used to swim across
to the island and back,
I was younger and happier then
walking up old 611, my towel
flung over my shoulder, my house lit up,
hungry, starving, for peach pie,
a little vanilla piled on, dear Rossky.

Acknowledgments

The new poems in this volume have appeared or will appear in the following journals:

American Poetry Review: "No Kissing There," "Hearts Amiss," "Wet Peach," "Under Your Wing," "Knucklebones," "Frutta da Looma," "Punching Holes"

Birmingham Review: "Baby Rat," "The Cost of Love," "March 17th"

Five Points: "Red and Swollen"

The New Yorker: "Adonis," "No House," "Warbler"

Plume: "Lake Country"

Poetry Magazine: "Cherries," "Hebrish," "Torn Coat"

I'd like to thank my editor, Jill Bialosky, and her assistant, Drew Weitman, for their guidance and support. I also want to thank my partner, Anne Marie Macari, and my assistant, Chase Berggrun, for their endless help and support.

Index of Titles and First Lines